Simply
Road Cycling

Peter Roxburgh

First Edition 2018

First Published 2018

ISBN 978-1-9993275-0-7

www.roxramblings.com

Nirvana, I dedicated a book to your mother when she was a little girl. Now, this one's for you

To Anya

From Mags & Jon

(p. 115: Descending was really useful when I had to re-learn the skills!)

xx

Simply Road Cycling

Contents

Simply Road Cycling

Introduction

Growing up in the West Midlands I found myself an oddball, an outsider. Most of my friends, inspired by Aston Villa, West Brom, and Wolves played football. I rode a bike. The peace and tranquillity of the Shropshire lanes and the adventure of discovering far off villages filled my time. Life was simple, and it was good.

Fast forward twenty years and I'd become another work obsessed thirty something in desperate need of losing a few pounds, well 70 of them in fact. Suddenly afflicted with heart palpitations, I sought the counsel of my local old-school doctor. The news wasn't catastrophic, but equally it wasn't great. I had no permanent damage - good. But, with blood pressure almost off the scale, unless I radically changed by lifestyle, my chances of seeing my 40th weren't great and my 50th? Almost an improbability the doc informed me. So goodbye booze and takeaways, hello bike.

Reunited after all those years, we got along just fine. The more I spent time with the bike, the more it rewarded me by decreasing my blood pressure and shedding the pounds. But, as I progressed to riding with others, I realised that times had changed, and I'd forgotten so much from my well spent youth. Bikes now had more than five gears, nutrition was no longer a Mars Bar and a banana sandwich, and equipment had become seemingly space-age.

I joined a cycling club, asked questions and I read - a lot. I changed career, retraining as a bike mechanic. I searched for nuggets of information, anything to make me a better rider. The more I learned, the more I wanted to learn. I wanted to know and be all things cycling.

Mission now accomplished, I feel a sense of duty to share my hard-earned knowledge so that others can benefit without investing hundreds, if not thousands, of hours in learning what it is to become a road cyclist. This book takes you, or any new or novice rider, on a journey that will, ultimately, enable you to become a seasoned and knowledgeable road rider.

Enjoy and I hope to see you on the road soon,

Peter

Palma de Mallorca, Spring 2018

Choosing a Road Bike

Congratulations, you're ready to take the plunge and buy your first road bike! It's an exciting time, but once you start browsing the lines of your local bike shop, it becomes abundantly clear that it's not an altogether straightforward task. What to buy? How much to spend? What extras to buy? There are so many questions whizzing around your head that it can almost seem overwhelming. Fear not: in this chapter we'll explore all things related to buying your first road bike.

> *"Get a bicycle.*
> *You will certainly not regret it,*
> *if you live."*
>
> Mark Twain

What to Buy

The first thing to consider is that you are buying a road bike - not a hybrid, not a mountain bike and definitely not a folding bike. A road bike is designed to allow you to travel the maximum amount of distance, in the minimum amount of time, with huge amounts of pleasure. It's characterised by skinny tyres (23 to 28 mm) and a drop handlebar (look at Figure 1 if you don't know what this is!).

Now, don't be fooled. Some websites and stores sell items that outwardly appear to be road bikes - they are not. The starting price for a road bike is in the region of £500. If what's on offer is less than this, you'll find that it compromises in so many ways: it will be clunky, heavy and no fun whatsoever to ride - your cycling career will end before it's barely begun (you've been warned). Equally, don't be bowled over by the shiny top-end models where prices rival that of a family car - they're all too much, too soon.

Figure 1 A drop handlebar

Frames & Forks

So, the first lesson is over and it's time to move onwards into the nitty gritty. The essence of a bike is its frame. Every component can change but the bike remains the same machine - change the frame and the bike becomes another. Frames are made of many materials, some very common such as aluminium and others far more exotic, such as bamboo. At the moment, you should concentrate on only two materials: aluminium and carbon. Ignore people (even those that are purportedly in the know) that warn you off one material or the other - they're living in the stone age. Both materials are light and, assuming an acceptable level of quality, ride well. The big difference is that carbon frames are normally lighter, give a more comfortable ride and most importantly, they are stiffer. Simply put, more of your power will go to the back wheel with carbon and this equates to more speed and faster climbing. In a nutshell, if you can afford it, buy carbon (expect prices to start at £1,000).

It's worth noting that frames and forks are not necessarily always made of the same materials. This is virtually always a reflection of price point. Almost all bikes beyond the absolute entry-level have carbon forks (it's the best material), but as a compromise to price points, some cheaper models will have forks made of other materials. Unless you really cannot afford anything else, avoid non-carbon forks - they're less responsive and heavier. Of course, you can always change the fork in the future, but this is not cheap and really is a false economy.

Another important aspect of a frame is its geometry. Geometry refers to the angles and lengths of all the tubes that together form the frame. It has a massive influence on the ride and handling of a bike. Cycle manufacturers publish specifications that detail the geometry of their bikes. These contain plenty of information, but don't be tempted to get wrapped up in the world of wheelbase lengths, chainstay shortness and head angles. You will only drive yourself crazy and still be none the wiser when it comes to making a good choice. In a nutshell, longer bikes with slacker head angles are more stable and as a result, will descend better. The flipside is that they are less responsive and reactive. Luckily, most manufacturers supply bikes in two geometries: race and endurance. As you're starting off, choose endurance. You'll find the position more comfortable because the handlebar is higher and closer to you without that classic racer-style drop from the saddle to the bars, and the handling will be confidence inspiring.

Groupsets

After the frame, the next thing that will jump out at you is the groupset. The groupset consists of all the mechanical elements of the bike, namely:

- Brakes
- Shifters
- Chain & Cassette

- Chainset
- Derailleurs

There are three main manufacturers of groupsets: Shimano, Campagnolo and SRAM. All of them make good equipment and once you are beyond your first bike, a choice becomes nothing more than a personal preference - just to illustrate this point, they are all present in the Tour de France. Each has its attributes that appeal to different riders:

- Shimano - fluid, smooth and parts are widely available. Most new bikes are Shimano equipped.
- Campagnolo - the original, more exclusive, and has a more mechanical feel.
- SRAM - the new kid on the block with its love-hate DoubleTap gear change system.

Groupsets belong to ranges such as Shimano 105 or Shimano Ultegra (better quality and lighter than 105). Each range will sport a certain number of speeds, namely how many gears appear at the back of the bike. Current groupsets range from eight to twelve speeds. The more gears you have the less of a jump there is between gears and this equates to a smoother, more comfortable ride. Table 1 shows current groupsets from the 'big three':

> **Good to Know:** To compare the size of different gear combinations, cyclists often use 'gear inches'. Gear inches are a throwback to the early days of cycling and express the size of a gear in terms of a penny farthing's wheel. The larger the number of the inches, the harder the gear.

If you have a keen eye, you'll notice that in many cases, bikes have a mixture of components from different groupsets and often the brakes may not belong to a groupset you recognise. This is generally because manufacturers create bikes to fit certain price points. They know that upgrading derailleurs to a

Manufacturer	Groupset	No. Speeds
Shimano	Claris	8
	Sora	9
	Tiagra	10
	105	11
	Ultegra (mechanical or electronic)	11
	Dura-ace (mechanical or electronic)	11
Campagnolo	Veloce	10
	Centaur	11
	Athena	11
	Potenza	11
	Chorus (mechanical or electronic)	11
	Record (mechanical or electronic)	12
	Super Record (mechanical or electronic)	12
SRAM	Apex	10
	Rival	11
	Force	11
	Red (mechanical or electronic)	11

Table 1 Groupsets by manufacturer

Note:
Electronic groupsets are those where gear changes are made by servos in the derailleurs rather than through the pull of a wire.

higher groupset whilst downgrading the brakes will catch the eye of many shoppers who can't resist having a bike with a swanky high end groupset - even if it is only the rear derailleur. You can, in the future, upgrade groupset components on your bike with the limitations being that they must come from a range with the same number of speeds and be from the same manufacturer. For example, if you buy a bike with Shimano 105, you can upgrade any of its components to Shimano Ultegra (both are 11 speed). Furthermore, you can upgrade your brakes to those of any groupset because they are not part of the bike's transmission. It's worth noting that occasionally, other factors affect compatibility, so you should always check with a mechanic or your local bike shop before buying new components.

OK, you've discovered lots of information about groupsets, but what does this mean in terms of choosing a bike? There are many variables at play, but there are a few key things that you really want to take onboard. Firstly, the more speeds you have the smoother the gear changes and the easier it is to upgrade components in the future. Secondly, groupsets below ten speed tend to feel a little clunky - if you can, avoid them. Thirdly, avoid buying outside of the 'big three' manufacturers. Although there are some high-quality alternatives on the market, there are also some poor ones - you'll be entering unchartered territory and it's too late for help!

It's worth noting that unless you have a custom-built bike, the components on a given model are specified by the manufacturer and the bike comes as shipped. Although you may not be able to choose specific components, you may be left with the dilemma of whether you should choose a better groupset with an aluminium frame, or a lesser groupset with a carbon frame? It's a tricky question and everyone will have their own take on it. Generally speaking, revert to aluminium if choosing carbon means dropping below eleven speed or 10 speed in Campagnolo world.

Other Components

After frames and groupsets, you move onto the other components which will make up your new bike. These components consist of a wheelset and finishing kit (bars, stem, saddle and seatpost). Of these, the wheelset makes the biggest difference to the ride and it consists of the following:

- Wheels, which are made up of rims, spokes, hubs, bearings and rim-tape
- Tyres & inner tubes

The individual components that make up a wheel affect its characteristics: stiffness, weight, resistance, durability and speed. If you have deep pockets, you can buy wheels that are specific to a given discipline - for example, ultra-light climbing wheels or deep-section aero wheels for time trialling (an individual race against the clock - more on this in the "Moving Forward: Your Next Steps" chapter). As a wheel becomes more specific, the price rises and a pair of wheels can easily cost more than your first bike. Don't panic. The good news is that any entry-level bike will come equipped with a reasonable pair of basic wheels. It's almost certain that they'll be nothing special but will get you rolling. In the future, worry about wheels. Invest in a good pair and they'll take your bike and your riding to the next level. For now, just accept the wheels shipped with your bike.

Ironically, new bikes often ship with awful tyres even though they are the only contact points between the bike and the road as shown in Figure 2. Just like wheels, tyres are made for specific purposes: weight, puncture protection, rolling resistance and price. Unlike wheels, tyres don't cost the earth. Ask the retailer to give you an honest opinion of their view on the tyres that come with your chosen bike. If they rate them, go with it - you can always change them in the future. If they don't, ask their advice - make sure you say if puncture protection is important to you (it's OK to be filled with dread when it comes to mending a puncture on the roadside - just don't admit it!). To give you an indication, expect to pay between £60 and £100 pounds for a pair of quality tyres.

Figure 2 Tyres are the only contact point between the bike and the road

Moving away from the rolling parts of the bike to the more sedate, stationary parts – the finishing kit. The finishing kit comprises of all of the remaining components of the bike, namely: saddle, seatpost, handlebar, stem and bar tape. Normally, you don't choose these components as they are specified by the manufacturer. In the future, you may want to change some of the finishing kit to improve your position on the bike or to upgrade to higher specification components. Notably, the handlebar and saddle, together with pedals, form your contact points with the bike. How your body interacts with these will make a huge difference to your riding comfort - or agony! As you advance your cycling career, investing in a quality bike-fit can be a great idea and it should increase both your performance and comfort whilst keeping you injury free. At the moment though, spending a couple of hundred pounds on a fit may be a little too much. So, instead, ask your retailer what kind of complimentary fit they offer - if they offer nothing, perhaps you need to be looking elsewhere. Of course, you can make your own adjustments following the advice in the "Getting the Right Fit" chapter.

Good to Know: Most road bikes have wheelsets that use tyres and inner tubes. The tyres in this type of system are known as clinchers. There are a growing number of road bikes that now adopt a tubeless system, which originated with mountain bikes. This system has no inner tube and requires a special tyre, rim and a liquid sealant that sits in the cavity between the tyre and rim. The benefits of tubeless systems include less punctures and more speed by removing the friction between inner tube and tyre. On the flip side, tubeless tyres tend to be heavier and fitting is more complicated than traditional clinchers.

You may also hear people talk about tubular tyres (tubs), which are not to be confused with tubeless. The tub is a specialist type of tyre with a sewn in inner tube and one where the entire assembly is glued to the wheel's rim. These tyres are very lightweight and can take high pressures making them popular with professionals, but their fitment makes them an unpopular choice for the rest of the world.

Good to Know: Saddles or razor blades as many customers call them, are supposed to be that shape - they are not an armchair. As you move from an upright riding position to a racing position, the rotation of your sit bones and your weight distribution change and a road saddle is designed to support you in this position.

Which Size is For You

The size of a bike refers to the size of its frame and these come in different sizes to suit riders of different heights and proportions. With current road bikes, the size will either be expressed as a measurement, such as 54 cm, or adjectively, such as Medium. It's important to remember that each manufacturer builds with their own geometry and frame design, so sizes do not always translate from one manufacturer to another. In other words, don't jump on to your mate's 56 cm Trek, find it a lovely fit, and then order a 56 cm Dolan - you would be in for a huge surprise, they're very different. Equally, you may be tempted to buy based on a manufacturer's own size charts and on face value, this may seem a good idea. However, although these can provide a good starting point, they are based on average rider proportions, an expected riding style and ignore physical characteristics such as flexibility or chronic injury. To establish exactly what size frame is going to work for you, you need to explore the basics of bike fit (see the next chapter: "Getting the Right Fit") and then apply these techniques to different frames and bikes until you are happy.

When to Buy

You want to buy now - right? Well, of course you do. However, if you're in the lucky position of having a loan bike or are not in a rush to buy, you can choose when to buy. Most of the cycle industry operates on a September (sometimes August) year start, where the manufacturers roll out their new models. If you want the absolute latest machine, you'll need to act fast as many of the most popular models quickly sell out and you may have to wait several weeks until a new shipment arrives. On the other hand, if you love a bargain, you'll see the sale stickers pop-up as late autumn approaches. If you're on a budget, this can be a great time to buy because discounts typically range from 10% to 30%.

Perhaps, you're only happy if you get an absolute steal - read on if this is you, but still, shame on you. The quietest time of year for bike shops is January and February. Add to this that many retailers are faced with huge bills for their Christmas stock (yes, Santa still brings kids bikes) and you have the perfect recipe for a deal. Always visit during mid-week for maximum effect - Saturdays are always busy, Mondays are workshop incoming days and Fridays are full of anticipation for the weekend ahead. Go for the deal, but don't be offended if the answer's no. At the end of the day, everyone has to make a living and margins on new bikes are not huge.

> **Good to Know:** We all like a deal, but it never feels great when people try to grind you down on price when margins are slim. So, instead of asking for a straight discount, ask for X value of accessories, clothing or future workshop time. These all cost the retailer less than a straight discount, yet the net result in your pocket is the same.

Where to Buy

Cycling is popular and new bike sales are up - 3.5 million in the UK alone in 2016! As a result, there are plenty of places where you can buy. Before exploring these, note that if you buy from a supermarket or catalogue, you'll only have yourself to blame - you'll find no friends here. Moving onwards to look at your choices and their pros and cons:

Online

There are plenty of big online retailers such as Wiggle and Chain Reaction, who offer great ranges of bikes often at very competitive prices. Obviously, choice, price and home delivery are great advantages. On the other hand, you don't really get to see what you're buying, you can't try it and it's a pain when things go wrong and you have to ship your bike back to the retailer. Most importantly though, you are choosing a bike size from a size-chart. This may work for you, but equally, you may be disappointed.

Also online, there are several direct sales manufacturers such as Ribble, Planet X and Dolan. These offer many of the benefits of other online retailers but with the big advantage that they're not paying a cut to the retailer. In most cases, these direct sales outfits offer a level of customisation that other retailers cannot. For example, you may be able to choose finishing kit, wheelset, groupset and even gear ranges. The obvious disadvantages are those of online retailers.

The High Street

Almost every town of any size has one of the big brands such as Halfords or Evans Cycles. These companies move huge numbers of bikes and can offer some good deals (at key times) that rival online, and for some there's the security of dealing with a big business. Being on the high street, it's simple to pop in store if you have a problem or simply want some advice. If you're fortunate, you'll also have the guidance and help of someone that actually knows what they are doing. Equally, the demand for staff means that many companies hire some people that are simply inexperienced or would not be able to survive in the world of independent retailers.

Which brings us nicely to independents, namely the Local Bike Shop (LBS as they're known). Local bikes shops vary massively in terms of size and offering. You'll need to ask in your local area to find out where road cyclists go - they'll all have an opinion. If you find a good shop, you'll have a choice of manufacturers and expert help on hand. A good shop will guide you through the buying process and do their utmost to find the bike that is the best for you. After you've bought, they'll always be there for after-service, warranty issues, advice and upgrades. If your local bike shop's not good, move on and find another - it's that simple.

Which Extras

Buying your first road bike is just the start, you've now entered a new world of equipment, parts and clothing. We'll explore clothing in the "Selecting the Right Gear: What to Wear" chapter, but for now let's discover the absolute essential kit that'll make you a road rider. Before you even leave the shop (assuming that you've been swayed back to the high street), you'll need the following:

- Two water bottle cages (you may only need one at the moment, but two says to the world that you're normally clocking up big miles). These are a universal fit, so don't worry - get the shop to pop them on for you - it's all part of the service.

- Two water bottles - your choice, but make sure that they don't clash with your frame colour.

- Spare inner tube - even if you can't change a tube yet, someone out there will help you. Note that inner tubes come in different sizes, you'll need 700 (diameter) by 23-28 (width, just ensure that it covers your tyre size).

- Tyre levers - don't be tempted to use spoons. Metal levers will wreck your rims and you'll be quickly buying new wheels...ouch!

- Hand pump - this'll pop in to a jersey pocket or attach directly to your frame under one of the bottle cages. Make sure that it is rated for the correct pressure, i.e. at least 110 PSI (other bikes require much lower pressures).

- A small multi-tool - at the moment it doesn't matter if you know what to do with it, it's just good form to have one rather than to borrow other people's.

- Storage for bits and pieces - you need something to store your tube, levers, multitool, cash and keys. You have a choice: a tool-tub, which is similar to a water bottle and fits in your bottle holder, or a saddlebag, which sits underneath your saddle (funnily enough). If you go for the latter, make it a micro/small one - you're not a touring cyclist, you're a road cyclist and you don't need to take the kitchen sink with you!

These are the essentials that fit on the bike, but there are a couple of items that you also need to keep at home. The first is chain lube. Even if you never plan to clean your bike, you must keep a small amount of lube on the chain otherwise it will squeak, squeal and slow you down...also a brown chain looks disgusting. The second item, although not absolutely essential, is a track pump. This kind of pump is a large hand operated pump and it offers the advantage of allowing you to check your tyre pressures before each ride with the minimum amount of effort. Without a track pump, you'll never get your tyres to their full pressure - yes, your handpump says 110PSI, but you'll end up with arms like Popeye just trying.

Rounding Up

In this chapter, you've learnt what makes a road bike a road bike, and you've learnt about the key components that constitute a bike. You've then received some top tips on where and when to buy, and which extras you need to buy. Before you rush out and make that all too pressing purchase, hold back and read the next chapter, which will ensure that you buy the correct sized bike.

Getting the Right Fit

Bike fit is a specialised discipline within the bike industry where tiny adjustments in a rider's position can equate to performance gains or loses. Equally, changes in position can affect the comfort of a rider, alleviate discomfort for existing physical ailments and drastically reduce the likelihood of a rider becoming injured. For any rider with problems, such as chronic knee or back conditions, a bike fit with an experienced fitter is a must. For everyone else, a good bike fit can be of real benefit, but not a necessity.

"It's all about being sat on the bike right."

Jason Rourke (Artisan Frame Builder)

By reading this book, it's unrealistic to expect to learn the intricacies and skills of a qualified bike fitter. However, you will learn how to choose your correct sized frame and how to make basic adjustments that will help you in terms of comfort, performance and efficiency.

Fundamentals of Fit

The first rule of bike fit is that it doesn't refer to making the rider fit the bike, but it conversely makes the bike fit the rider. This is an important concept to take onboard - it's really not nice to start chopping or sticking bits to a rider. The second rule is that the bike has to be the right size to start with. Although a good fitter can adjust almost any bike to be rideable by any rider, if the frame is not the right size to start with, the end result will always be a compromise, not a great ride and frequently, not pleasing to the eye. If you follow the advice outlined in this chapter, you'll quickly and easily be able to see and feel whether a particular bike is the right size for you.

When fitting a bike to a rider, it helps to think of a fit consisting of three key elements (Figure 3), these being:

1. The Foundation - feet and pedals form the foundation from which the rest of the bike fit will take place.

2. The Backend - saddle height, fore and aft position (explained later) and angle are key to gaining maximum performance and efficiency.

3. The Frontend - stem length and handlebar size and position all impact both the comfort and performance of the rider.

Figure 3 Three elements of bike fit

The Foundation: Pedals and Feet

Pedals and feet form the foundation from which the rest of the bike fit will take place. A good fitter will spend a significant proportion of their time focusing on a client's feet to ensure a solid foundation. This is because subtle changes at the foot level can have profound effects further up the rider's legs and, as a result, impact their pedalling comfort and efficiency. Professional fitters use a number of items to fine tune this foundation, such as: footbeds, shims, cleat wedges and pedal spacers. Their use is beyond the scope of this book because if performed without complete knowledge, they can easily result in overuse or chronic injury. For now, you need to ensure two things: the first is that you have the correct size shoes and the second is that any cleats that you fit to your shoes are positioned correctly. You'll learn all about shoes and cleats in the "Shoes" section of the "Selecting the Right Gear: What to Wear" chapter.

The Backend: Saddle Position & Height

Fitting the backend of the bike is all about the efficient and safe production of rider power. There are three elements that together, form the backend fit:

1. Saddle Angle and Alignment.
2. Saddle Height.
3. Saddle Fore and Aft Position.

Saddle Angle and Alignment

Saddle angle and alignment are the simplest elements of backend fit. The saddle must point directly forward. If it is skewed and offline, it will chafe the rider and push their hips into an unnatural angle which will eventually lead to injury. To check saddle alignment, stand behind the bike and look along the saddle and ensure that it is perfectly in line with the top-tube of the frame – see Figure 4. If it's not, adjust it until it is right.

Traditionally, a saddle should be absolutely level, as shown in Figure 5, because it is designed to support a rider's sit bones when in this position. A saddle that points downwards will push the rider's weight on to their hands, often resulting in numb hands and aching wrists. Conversely, a saddle that points upwards will exert pressure on the genital area which will result in numbness and discomfort. Additionally, an upwards pointing saddle will allow the rider to slide gradually backwards making it harder for them to control the bike and cause stress in their upper body from hanging on to the handlebar. All of this said, there are two exceptions to the level saddle rule:

1. Some time-triallists and triathletes point their saddles slightly downwards to compensate for their very forward positions on their bikes. This is not something to emulate on a normal road bike.

2. Some women suffer discomfort where they really don't want discomfort. A very slight downward tilt (1 degree) may alleviate this discomfort.

> **Good to Know:** Eddy Merckx, generally considered the greatest road cyclist ever, famously used to use a spirit level, a long metal ruler and a tape measure so that he could ensure that his saddle was exactly in position. He was known to stop during a race to make on the fly adjustments!

Saddle Height

So often, when a first-time road rider goes for a fitting, they're surprised by the height of the saddle: "How high?" they exclaim, "I can't put my feet on the floor!". Of course, the basic idea of riding a bike is that you pedal it rather than scoot along by foot. Seriously though, a lot of people ride with a saddle that is far too low. You'll spot them on the road all the time: their knees move outwards with each turn of the pedals and their legs barely seem to extend beyond ninety degrees. These people are doing themselves a great injustice because they're making it very hard work to pedal, are completely inefficient and, ultimately, are setting themselves up for serious knee injuries.

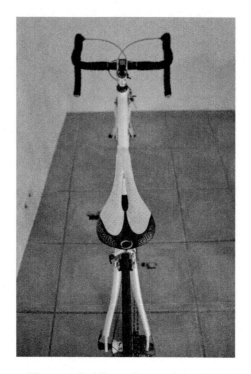

Figure 4 Saddle and top tube in line

Figure 5 A level saddle

At the other end of the spectrum, there are people that have saddle positions that are far too high. Again, you'll see them out on the road. Their riding style is characterized by toes that point downwards during the entire pedal stroke as they struggle to reach the bottom of the pedal stroke and they shift at the pelvis from side to side as they pedal. This shifting or tilting of the pelvis can create serious wear on the hip joints, which with enough time and distance, will result in chronic injury.

There are a number of established methods for attaining correct saddle height. Each method results in a slightly different saddle height, but this is not a problem because rather than there being one definitive saddle height for a rider, there is actually an acceptable range - although this only covers a few millimetres up to perhaps one centimetre. Methods that are commonly used include:

25 to 35 Degree Method - your upper and lower leg form an angle, at maximum pedal extension, of between 145 to 155 degrees. This requires a goniometer to measure angles. Professional bike fitters commonly use variations of this method when performing a bike fit.

The LeMond Method - inseam multiplied by 0.883 equals height from middle of saddle to the centre of the bottom bracket as shown in Figure 7. To measure your inseam (Figure 6), stand upright against a wall and position a book between your legs. Have an assistant measure down from the top of the book to the floor – this is your inseam. Example calculation:

85 cm (inseam) * 0.883 = 75.1 cm saddle height

The 109% Method - inseam multiplied by 109% equals height from middle of the saddle to the centre of the crank's pedal spindle – see Figure 8. Measure your inseam as you did for the

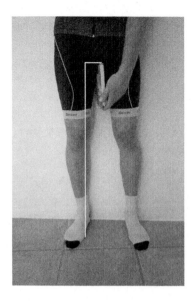

Figure 6 Measuring inseam

Figure 7 Applying Saddle Height Using the LeMond Method

LeMond method. Multiply inseam by 109% to calculate saddle height. Example calculation:

> *85 cm (inseam) * 109% = 92.7 cm saddle height*

Heel to Pedal Method - extend your leg fully and it should just skim the pedal as shown in Figure 9.

Use one or more of these methods to establish your saddle height. Pop the saddle up to the correct height and then, with either someone supporting the bike or with the bike fixed into a stationary trainer, jump on and see how the height feels. Unless you made an error in your calculations, you should feel neither over-reached or unable to gain a nice leg extension.

Before you take the bike for a spin, you'll want to adjust the saddle fore and aft (see the next section) and after this, you'll need to recheck that the saddle height is correct. This is because moving the saddle backwards or forwards will alter the effective height of the saddle. Once you're happy with the saddle height, you can do a couple of things to make sure that the final height is right for you. The first is to ask someone to watch from behind as you pedal and ensure that your hips don't rock. If they do, you'll need to lower your saddle until they no longer rock or move from side to side. The second thing that you can do is go for a ride. It's natural that your body will go through a period of adjustment to your position on the bike, but there are certain clues that can suggest an incorrect saddle height:

- Pain radiating from the front of the knee can suggest a saddle height that is too low.
- Pain behind the knee can suggest a saddle height that is too high.

Figure 8 Applying saddle height using the 109% method

Figure 9 Heal to pedal method

- Excessive muscular pain in your quadriceps (front leg muscles) can suggest a saddle height that is too low.
- Excessive muscular pain in your hamstrings (rear leg muscles) can suggest a saddle height that is too high.

Saddle Fore and Aft

The saddle fore and aft, how far forward or backward it sits on its rails, is one of the most misunderstood aspects of saddle adjustment. There are many people that move the saddle to adjust their reach on the bike, in other words to move themselves closer or further away from the handlebar. Although moving the saddle affects the rider's reach, this is a side effect and not the reason to move it. The actual reason to move the saddle is to change the angle and position of your legs as they turn the pedals. Figure 10 shows two extreme examples of saddle position and how they affect pedal stroke. Notice that the rider on the right is pushing the pedal away from them – not an efficient use of their muscles - whereas the rider on the left is so far forward that their knee is flexing well forward of the pedal. Flexing the knee at this point is similar to performing a squat with knees forward of the feet. This will create a large amount of pressure on the kneecap, which will ultimately result in an injury.

The traditional method for establishing fore and aft is known as KOPS (Knee Over Pedal Spindle). To set the saddle position using this method, the rider sets the pedals at the three and nine o'clock positions. An assistant drops a plumb-line from the bony protrusion under the knee cap and aims to have the plumb-bob line up directly with the pedal spindle, as shown in Figure 11. For the majority of riders, this method results in an acceptable to ideal position. However, there are some riders where this method does not give the best results. A professional bike fitter may utilise a number of techniques to establish fore and aft, but these require specialist tools.

Figure 10 Extreme fore and aft saddle positions

Figure 11 Knee Over Pedal Spindle (KOPS)

Another approach to set fore and aft is to initially use KOPS and then either video yourself on a static trainer or ask an assistant to watch you pedal. Your lower leg should never reach an absolute vertical angle or surpass it so that your foot is pointing forward during the pedal stroke. Equally, you'll know that the saddle is too far forward if your knee extends past the pedal spindle at any point during the pedal revolution.

When on the road cycling, there are some clues to incorrect saddle positions. One of the best physical tests is to climb a long hill so that your legs are under stress and more likely to signal any problems. If your quadriceps scream as you climb, there's a good chance you've gone too extreme with the forward position. Equally, if you're aching or feeling pain in your hamstring, glutes or lower back, there's a good chance that you're too far back. You'll probably notice that these signs are similar to incorrect saddle height, so you'll need to make sure that you're happy with that first. When you do make changes, only make small ones and one at a time. This way you won't shock your body with the differences, and you'll know which are positive changes and which are not. After your initial setup, limit changes to no more than 2 mm to avoid physical adaption problems.

The Frontend: Handlebar Position and Stem Length

The backend of the bike fit was all about power and efficiency, the frontend concerns comfort and aerodynamic performance. These two aspects are often opposing features. As the rider becomes more aerodynamic, they become less comfortable and inversely, more comfort usually results in less aerodynamic gain. Every bike fitter's aim is to deliver the perfect balance between comfort and performance for a given rider. In practical terms, as the handlebar rises and gets closer to the

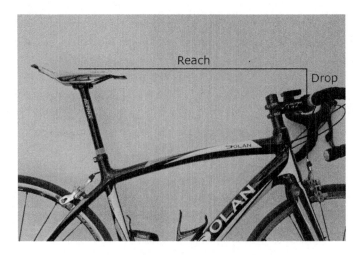

Figure 12 Handlebar reach and saddle-to-bar drop

Figure 13 Aligning handlebar and hub to establish reach

rider, the greater the comfort and, naturally, as they lower and move away from the rider, the aerodynamic gain increases.

Regardless of where on the comfort-performance spectrum you aim to arrive, you'll be working with two variables: handlebar reach (reach) and saddle to bar drop (drop). In this section, consider reach to be the distance from the seated rider to the handlebar, and drop as the difference in height between the saddle and the handlebar. Figure 12 illustrates reach and drop:

Reach will affect your comfort and control of the bike. Too short a reach and you may hit your knees on the handlebar when climbing out of the saddle and because your weight will be disproportionately over the front wheel, you'll find it hard to control the bike as you descend. Too long a reach and you'll suffer discomfort in your triceps and upper back, and you'll find that you seem to be hanging on to the handlebar because your arms will be unable to absorb the shocks of the road as they will be fully extended.

> **Good to Know:** Based on average proportions, women have relatively longer legs and shorter torsos than men. This means that they often require a shorter reach than men of the same height. Many new bikes don't reflect this requirement, so to the obtain the best fit, many women will require a shorter stem than the one shipped with their bikes – continue reading for more details.

Professional fitters often work on the angles formed by the upper and lower arms and between the torso and the upper arm. Luckily, there is an old-school technique that requires no special tools and produces very accurate results. Sit on the bike, put your hands in your normal riding position (generally on the hoods) and look straight down through the handlebar. If the handlebar obscures your view of the front wheel's hub (see Figure 13), the reach is correct. If you can see the hub clearly forward of the handlebar, the reach is too short. Conversely, if the hub is visible behind the handlebar, the reach is too long.

If you found that your reach was incorrect, you'll need to change the stem of your bike. Stems are relatively cheap components and are designed to be changed to suit the needs of riders. They are available in lengths from zero to 150 mm (occasionally more) in 10 mm increments. On a road bike, the stem should be between 60 mm and 130 mm. If you require a stem that is shorter or longer, you have a frame that is either too short or too long. Changing the stem is not a big job, but it is very important that it is done correctly because if performed incorrectly it can lead to a loss of steering whilst riding! Good bike shops will have a range of stems in stock and will happily changes yours for you, perhaps for a small charge - perhaps for free if you're a regular customer.

Now that the reach of the bike suits you, you need to ensure that the drop meets your riding style's requirements. Visualise a horizontal line starting from the saddle and passing over the handlebar. The vertical distance between this line and handlebar is the drop, as shown in Figure 12.

In simple terms, the greater the drop, the more aerodynamic you become and the smaller the drop, the more comfortable you'll find yourself. At the extremes, a classic touring position has zero drop (level saddle and handlebar), whereas a professional racer may have six inches of drop. Most recreational riders will benefit from a drop of between zero and 50 mm (two inches) as this offers a good balance between comfort and performance. Before you adjust 'drop', you must also consider your flexibility. An excessive drop coupled with poor flexibility will result in pain in the hamstrings and lower back and may result in a drop in power output. As a guide, a comfortable drop will be:

• Can't touch toes – zero drop.
• Finger tips touch toes – 25-50 mm (1-2 inches) of drop.

- Palms flat on the floor – 100-150 mm (4-6 inches) of drop.

To adjust the drop, assuming that you have a modern road bike, there are two approaches you can take. The first is to move the stem up and down the steering column by shifting spacers from above or below the stem, shown in Figure 14.

Figure 14 Spacers and stem height

The second approach is to change your bike's stem. As you discovered previously, stems are available in a variety of lengths and you can change them to adjust the fit of your bike. Stems also come in a variety of angles, typically from zero to 45 degrees. The angle of the stem will move the handlebar up or down depending on how it is fitted. If you so desire, some high school trigonometry will allow you to calculate the angle of stem to move the handlebar up or down by a given amount. In reality, it's much simpler to pop to a bike shop and explain what you want to achieve and try a few stems until you are happy with the result. Once you've achieved your desired drop, you'll need to recheck reach. This is because changes in drop, affect reach.

Rounding Up

In this chapter, you've learnt the fundamentals of bike fit and how it affects the comfort and performance of a rider. You've learnt how to maximise performance by correct saddle positioning and height. Finally, you've discovered how to balance aerodynamic performance and comfort by adjusting reach and handlebar height by changing your bike's stem.

Selecting the Right Gear: What to Wear

All sports have a range of clothing and footwear specifically designed for their participants. Sometimes, these items are obviously pretty essential (wetsuits for UK surfers springs to mind) and at other times, they are seemingly more fashion orientated - a strap on shark fin for swimmers...come on! In this chapter you'll discover not only which items of clothing are essential, but also, as some may argue, you'll learn what not to wear.

"To me, it doesn't matter whether it's raining or the sun is shining or whatever: as long as I'm riding a bike I know I'm the luckiest guy in the world."

Mark Cavendish

Absolute Essential Gear

In theory, you can cycle in any clothing of your choice...or none whatsoever, if that's your thing (check out the World Naked Bike Ride). That said, the correct clothing will make your ride more comfortable, more hygienic and faster. Unsurprisingly, there's a myriad of clothing to choose from, but some items are simply 'nice to have' or useful optional extras. The absolute essentials are:

- Shorts
- Technical top
- Socks
- Shoes
- Mitts
- Helmet
- Cycling glasses

Shorts

Road cycling shorts are made from Lycra (or a similar material) and have a padded interior to aid comfort and keep you hygienic. You may feel a little self-conscious wearing Lycra when you first start out and may feel tempted to wear a baggy over-short. If you feel the need to do this, fair enough. However, you'll quickly want to revert to Lycra because the additional drag from a baggy short will slow you down, and you're simply not going to look the part.

When choosing shorts, there are three key features to consider:

The first is the padding. Cheap shorts have a basic foam pad which provides some comfort, but which is prone to becoming saturated with moisture (sweat or rain). The next level of shorts provide a gel pad, which will not absorb moisture but will offer you a higher level of comfort. Beyond this, pads become more technical and not only will provide higher levels of comfort, but will also give a better fit and have antibacterial qualities - no-one wants to suffer from saddle sores!

The second feature is material. Almost all shorts will utilise Lycra (or a similar material) and this comes in different weights and may be mixed with other materials. Generally cheaper shorts are manufactured from thin materials and tend to lose their shape and wear through (in the saddle area) quite quickly.

Thirdly, and finally, shorts come as either shorts or bib-shorts (bibs). Normal shorts are the cheapest and pose no problems if you require a natural break (restroom stop). On the other hand, experienced riders will almost always opt for bibs because they do not constrict the waist, will always stay in position and do not create an exposed area if your jersey rides up, thus saving you a chilled back.

Whichever style and type of short you choose, there are three key things you should keep in mind:

1. Buy short legs - 1-2 inches above the top of the kneecap. Three quarter and full-length legs are available and are great to wear at certain times of the year, but with some clever clothing choices, they're not necessary in your initial wardrobe (see the "Warmers" section later in this chapter).
2. Keep them black. Flashes of colour or logos are perfectly acceptable and sometimes even look cool but shorts in a full colour are a bad move. That said, if you have the build of a professional cyclist, white or coloured shorts may look okay, but for the rest of the world, colours make your butt look big! Also, white shorts tend to become translucent in the wet, and a wet road will leave you sporting a very unflattering black stripe up your backside - you have been warned.
3. Stay au natural. Cycling shorts are designed to be worn without underwear. If you ride with underwear, do not be surprised if you chafe and feel very uncomfortable.

Good to Know: Some riders suffer terribly from a sore backside. Muscular pain is part of the process of your butt toughening up, but soft skin irritation is not. If you're a sensitive soul, search out chamois cream (online or good bike shops), which will ease your discomfort.

Technical Tops & Cycling Jerseys

A cotton t-shirt or similar will soon become saturated as you cycle - don't wear one. If your budget is really tight, simply wear a technical t-shirt like those sold for a couple of pounds in Decathlon. However, as soon as you can, invest in your first cycling jersey. The cycling jersey has a number of features that are specific to cyclists, namely:

1. The cut. A cycling jersey is short at the front and longer at the rear. This means that when you are in a hunched over cycling position, the top sits evenly on your torso.

2. Zips. There are three common lengths of zip, all of which make it easy to pop your top on and allow you to create extra ventilation when things start getting a little warm. There's a short zip, a medium zip and a full-length mountain climber's zip, which allows you to fully open the front of your jersey (only do this if you have the anorexic build of a pro cyclist - it's not nice to see a big belly bouncing off someone's knees as they pedal).

3. Pockets. Typically, a cycling jersey will have three pockets on the rear, which allow you to stash food, equipment and spare clothing. This means that you don't have to stop cycling to grab things and you'll not have to spoil the look of your bike by having a huge saddlebag.

Figure 15 Dressing well is important

Almost all cycling tops will have these features so your final choice will come to fit, feel and fashion. Once you start browsing, you'll see that there's a huge choice in terms of appearance - you can choose between team tops (Sky or BMC for example), those that promote a manufacturer (Specialized or Trek for example), quirky tops (skeletons or Marmite), trendy high-end designer tops and conversely, fairly bland utilitarian ones. The choice is yours, but a top tip is to avoid the World Champion's jersey (normally white with rainbow bands). Many club cyclists have an issue with people wearing the World Champ's top. Their argument is that only the World Champ should wear that top – after all, they're the only one that put the work in, won the race and therefore merit wearing the rainbow bands.

Figure 16 A bold sock statement

Socks

If ever there was a contentious issue, sock choice is a prime example of one. In the past, life was simple. Socks were white and sat 4-6 inches above the ankle bone. Then, Lance Armstrong broke with tradition and started wearing black socks - crazy! Oh, and of course, triathlon suddenly became cool and people started to ride with no socks whatsoever. And, as if things couldn't become any worse, the market became flooded with socks sporting all kinds of crazy designs and colours - a veritable Hawaiian shirt smorgasbord (Figure 16). Not only were people now riding with all kinds of socks, they started playing with the length too. Now, it's not unusual to see trainer socks that are virtually invisible once housed in a shoe and, even more disturbing, some people feel the need to wear socks that almost touch the knee - is this some kind of fetish or what?

There are some (author included) that stick with tradition. At the end of the day, white looks clean and neat and is, without a shadow of a doubt, faster than any other variant on the market. However, feel free to make your own choice but please keep the length appropriate. If you absolutely must wear some quirky length, do it in the privacy of your own home - thanks.

Shoes

Really this section should be entitled, "Shoes, Pedals and Cleats" because the three are bound together. When you start off cycling, you may simply ride in trainers with a flat pedal or a pedal with a toe-clip but you'll soon progress onto a clipless system (where your shoe is attached directly to the pedal in a similar way to a ski binding). There are a number of reasons that you'll want to progress to a clipless system, including:

1. Efficiency - more of your power will transmit into forward motion, which in turn means that you'll ride faster and climb more efficiently.
2. Safety - once your foot is directly connected to the pedal, it cannot move, accidently slip off the pedal or come into contact with a moving part of your bike.
3. Injury - because your foot is in an optimum pedalling position, assuming that the system is setup correctly, you are less likely to suffer soft tissue injury from bad positioning.
4. Energy - your lower leg muscles work less to stabilise your leg so you can ride for longer before these muscles tire.

A clipless system consists of three parts: pedals, cleats and shoes (see Figure 17). There are a number of different systems on the market and your choice of system dictates your choice of shoes, pedals and cleats. Starting with pedals, most can be split into one of two distinct styles: mountain bike or road. In all cases, a small cleat made of either metal or plastic bolts directly to the bottom of your shoe. This cleat clicks into the pedal mechanism to secure your feet to the pedals. Within this mechanism there is a spring, which when stressed (intentionally or in the event of an accident) will release the cleat from the pedal, thus freeing your foot from the bike.

Figure 17 Pedal, shoe and cleat

Good to Know: Although you are clipped in with a clipless system, they are known as 'clipless' systems because they do not have the old-fashioned toe-clip.

Mountain bike style pedals tend to have a small cleat made of metal (for durability), which is connected to the shoe by two bolts. Although, this style of pedal started life as something designed specifically for off-road riders, its popularity has significantly increased with road riders, especially those at the start of their careers. The advantages to the road rider include:

- Easy to clip in and out of - providing a sense of security.

- They have lots of float - your foot can move freely for several degrees in any direction, which means that the precise location of the cleat becomes less important.

- The cleats are located in a recess within the sole of the shoe, which means you can walk with ease.

- Pedals are often double sided, which allows you to clip in on either side, so you don't have to flip the pedal with your toe before clipping in.

Road bike style pedals tend to have a large cleat made of plastic, which is connected to the shoe through three bolts. More experienced road riders and those that take part in some form of competition, generally use this style of pedal. Although this style of pedal is less user-friendly than the mountain bike style (single-sided, hard to clip into and awkward to walk in), it does offer the rider a number of advantages, including:

- A larger cleat spreads the load of the foot reducing the chances of pressure points, creating a more comfortable ride over long distances.

- The larger cleat allows you to push more power through the drive train, which in turn will improve efficiency and performance.

- Looks more professional - shallow, but important to some.

If you intend to take part in any form of competition (time trialling, local races or even sportives), choose a road style system. On the other hand, if most of your riding will take the form of commuting or touring, perhaps a mountain bike system will be more appropriate. If you fall somewhere in between, it's up to you.

Once you've chosen the style of pedal system, you'll need to choose a pedal manufacturer. Not surprisingly, there are many manufacturers offering pedal systems, all of which claim to be better than any of their competitors. This said, the market is dominated by four main players:

- Shimano - in most countries Shimano absolutely dominates the market, which means that should you ever need a replacement pedal or cleat, you will find one easily.
- Look - popular in some European countries, Look offers a wide-range of pedals including the user-friendly Keo Easy for road riders.
- Time – in common with Look, Time's pedals are popular in some European countries.
- Speedplay - 'lollipop' style pedals make Speedplay's offerings easy to spot. They are exceptionally customisable but have a starting price that is much higher than many manufacturers.

Good to Know: In most cases, when you buy a pair of pedals they ship with cleats, so you don't have to buy these separately.

Good to Know: When you buy a road bike it will come with either no pedals or a pair of cheap flat pedals. It is assumed that road riders will have their own preference of pedal system.

Now that you have selected your pedal system, you can move on to choosing shoes. The first thing to ensure is that you select a shoe that has the correct number of bolt holes in the sole for the pedal system you have chosen, namely 2 bolts for mountain style, 3 bolts for road style or 4 bolts for Speedplay systems (Speedplay offers adapters that allow fitment to three bolt shoes). Then, as you move on to making a choice, it is likely to be driven initially by budget. Shoes tend to start at £50-60 and easily go up to £400. There are a number of reasons that the price increases, but the two most important ones are sole material and closure system.

Entry to mid-level shoes have a hardened plastic (or similar) sole, whereas higher-end ones have carbon soles. Plastic has a certain amount of flex and this flex will increase with time, but the flex in carbon is not visible to the human eye. You can test this for yourself, hold a plastic shoe in your hands and really try to bend it - you'll see a very small amount of movement – unless, of course, it's really cheap and then it'll bend like a banana. Now repeat the same process with a carbon soled shoe - see, no movement. Either sole material will allow you to get riding, let your budget dictate your choice.

Figure 18 Nice shoes

All shoes have to have some sort of closure systems, otherwise your feet would pop out as you pedal. Occasionally, this system will consist of laces, which may be because the shoe is aimed at touring riders or, conversely, is really fashionable. However, in most cases, the closure system will consist of straps, dials or a combination of the two. Basic straps attached via Velcro offer a simple and cheap closure system. More advanced straps will operate through a ratchet system, which allows a more precise fit and additional security because they're unlikely to come undone. At a higher price point, you'll see shoes that have dials that tighten or loosen what is, in effect, a wire lace. These systems offer total adjustability and security but are naturally more expensive.

Having selected a shoe, it's time to try it on because at the end of the day, if it doesn't fit you it's pointless. Just like any other style of shoe, sizing and width varies between manufacturer, so buying without trying is a lottery! So, how do you know if they fit? Don't start going for a walk around the store or performing squats or lunges or any other strange kind of moves. The cycling shoe is, as its name implies, for cycling - not walking. Firstly, does the shoe pinch or feel tight in any area? If so, this will only get worse as you ride because your feet swell as you exercise. Secondly, do your feet feel like they are flapping around inside the shoe, or that your toes have a long way to reach the end of the shoe? If so, cycling like this will cause you to scrunch your toes in an attempt to secure your foot, which in turn will place an unnecessary workload on your lower leg muscles. Try a couple of sizes and models; if nothing feels right, move on and try another store.

Mitts

Currently, there's a trend to ride with bare hands. It gives a tactile experience and, some would say, a liberating experience. If you've ridden so many miles that your hands are devoid of sensation and scarred so heavily from falls, riding with bare hands could be a good choice for you. On the other hand (excuse the pun), if you like to use your hands to feel and would prefer to keep them silky smooth, mitts are a good choice.

Cycling mitts are short fingered gloves designed specifically for cycling. They offer a snug, but not constrictive, fit and have strategically positioned padding on the palms. A good mitt will benefit you in many ways, including:

- Protect your hands in the case of a fall - picking gravel out of your palms is not fun.
- Provide shock absorption against road noise, reducing the chance of numb hands.
- Warm your hands a little, so that you can still use the brakes during a long descent.
- Offer a surface to wipe sweaty brows or running noses against – gross, but true!

When choosing a mitt, ensure a snug yet not restrictive fit - a loose fit will bunch up and blister your hands. Then take a look at the padding. Cheaper mitts have foam pads that with time, compress and absorb moisture whereas more expensive mitts use gel, which provides good cushioning and doesn't soak up moisture. Also, check between the fingers. Some mitts provide little tabs that allow you to pull your mitts off easily - a handy (yet another pun, sorry) feature. Finally, ensure that their colour and design does not clash with the rest of your clothing.

Helmet

There's a small group of people that prefer to ride without a helmet. Most of this group consists of hipsters, old men who never needed a helmet when they were lads and people that don't like to mess up their hair. Joking aside, there are people that ride without helmets and they have their reasons, such as:

- Hot head - helmets of the past were perhaps a little warm, but new ones make little difference.
- Looking silly - you're dressed in Lycra...get over yourself.
- Feel - some don't like the sensation of something on their head.
- Smell - helmets encase a sweaty head, which can lead to a pong. There are plenty of products to freshen smelly helmets and shoes too.

- Risk - perhaps the craziest reason. There are people that believe wearing a helmet increases your chances of hitting your head when you come off and that car drivers are more likely to hit a cyclist wearing a helmet...go figure!

The truth of the matter is that everyday people suffer fatalities or life changing injuries as a result of a head trauma and wearing a helmet drastically reduces the chances of such things.

Figure 19 A well fitted helmet

In most countries, all helmets will meet or exceed safety standards - this makes your life easier when making a choice. Expect to pay anything from £20 to £200 pounds for a helmet. The difference? As helmets increase in price, a number of their features and aspects of their construction change, notably:

- Specificity - entry-level helmets are aimed at recreational users and don't have features aimed at specific types of rider, for example, mountain bikers or road cyclists.

- Weight - all cycling helmets will feel light, but every gram is a gram that your neck must support as you ride. The higher the price, generally the lower weight.

- Venting - as helmets become more specific to a discipline and are manufactured with more advanced techniques and materials, the opportunities to increase ventilation increase. Generally, a more expensive helmet will keep your head cooler - especially important when climbing in summer.

- Protection - although they all meet safety standards, more expensive helmets will provide additional protection in the areas where a road strike is more likely.

Choose your price point and then try on a number of helmets to find one that provides a good fit, as shown in Figure 19. Almost all helmets are adjustable to the size of the user's head, but mid to high-end helmets additionally come in a range of sizes, which helps obtain the best possible fit.

To try on the helmet, pop it onto your head, ensuring that the front sits about one to two finger widths above your eyebrows. Adjust the tightening mechanism (usually a dial at the rear) and do up the chin strap so it's almost snug but in no way restrictive. The inside of the helmet should contact as much of your head as possible - large gaps between the top of your head and the helmet are not good. Try twisting the helmet. With enough force, you'll always be able to move it, but ensure that it doesn't twist or slide with little or no effort. If it does move, it'll do the same in the event of an accident. Next, assess the helmet for feel. You'll be aware that it's on your head, but there should be no pressure points and no part of it should feel like it's digging into your flesh. Finally, take a look in the mirror - it's vain, but you need to know that you look good.

Cycling Glasses

When leisure cycling, most people only sport eyewear as a fashion accessory or for protection against the sun. However, when road riding, protective eyewear becomes essential to protect your eyes against: the sun, the wind, and foreign objects (grit, insects, etc). With the speeds involved in road cycling, you'll find that the wind, especially during descents, will make your eyes water to the point where it becomes difficult to see. And, should an insect hit your eye at 40 mph, you'll discover a whole world of pain. Cycling eyewear is sport specific, so a standard pair of sunglasses, although offering some protection, are not appropriate. Well-constructed cycling eyewear has several features that makes it ideal for the road cyclist, such as:

- UV protection regardless of whether the lenses are clear or coloured.

- Ergonomic design that prevents fogging of the lenses through sweat.

- Full eye coverage that protects your eyes from foreign objects.

- Lenses that are strong enough to endure impacts from grit and stones thrown up from the road.

- A shape that deflects wind away from your eyes.

Just like regular sunglasses, cycling eyewear varies enormously in price. All legitimate eyewear will perform the same basic role, but more expensive varieties may offer additional features, for example:

- Improved frame material.
- Enhanced lens coatings.
- Higher levels of impact protection.
- Adjustable/flexible arms and nose piece.
- Differing lens types, such as photochromatic.
- Premium brand.

Whatever price point and whichever brand you chose, your starting point is to establish your riding conditions. Eyewear comes with different lenses to suit different light conditions. Consider the difference in light conditions between a drizzly UK winter's day and a sun-drenched afternoon in Spain – the same lenses aren't really going work that well. The main types of lenses are:

- Clear – for flat light.
- Orange or yellow – enhance low light.
- Tinted or darkened – for progressively bright conditions.
- Photochromatic – adjust to light conditions.
- Changeable – you can change the lenses to suit the conditions.

Once you've chosen a lens type, try the eyewear on to make sure that it fits well and suits you. The eyewear needs to cover your eyes properly, feel comfortable and fit securely. Beyond lens choice and fit, it's your choice of which additional features or brand you want to adopt. It's also worth considering that if you intend to use the same eyewear for riding off road, it will take far more abuse (mud, stones, etc) and is far more likely to get lost.

Good to Know: If you normally wear prescription glasses, you may find that wearing them to ride is problematic because they can slide around, not give you full eye coverage and steam up when climbing. There are a few options that will allow you to protect your eyes and see too – a real bonus! The first is to wear contact lenses and normal cycling eyewear. Daily disposable contacts have become very cheap and because they are made of a very thin material, they are far more comfortable than traditional variants. The second is to invest in prescription sports eyewear. This is a relatively expensive alternative to contacts, but for those that can't take to lens, it is a viable option.

Almost Essential Gear

If you only ever intend to ride on warm sunny days, you don't need to read this section. If on the other hand, you're willing to run the risk of riding on days where it may be a little chilly or wet, you need to read on. In this section, you'll discover the extra items of clothing that allow experienced riders to ride in comfort whatever the weather has to throw at them.

Warmers: Leg, Arm, Head, Neck and Knee

Warmers are some of the most important additions to your cycling wardrobe, they allow you to mix and match outfits depending on weather conditions, and allow you to add or remove garments to regulate your temperature during rides. They are all generally made of Lycra (or a similar material) or a fabric containing Lycra, so are lightweight and provide a snug fit. The following are the types of warmer that you're likely to see in any good bike shop:

- Leg warmers - cover your leg from upper thigh to just above the ankle. A great item that may save you from ever buying full length cycling shorts.

- Arm warmers - cover your arm from just below the armpit to just above the wrist. Of all the types of warmer, these are the most frequently used because your arms are stationary when you ride and easily chill. The great things about arm warmers are that they are small, stuff easily into a pocket and, with experience, are simple to take on and off as you ride.

- Skull cap - a very thin, light and brimless cap that forms a covering between your head and the inside of your helmet. An item that will keep your head amazingly warm!

- Neck warmer - a simple tube of material that covers your neck, which amazingly makes a huge difference to how warm you feel. Unlike, the other warmers, neck warmers are loose fitting – for an obvious reason.

- Knee warmers - cover a region that extends approximately 8-10 inches either side of your knee. You can use these warmers throughout most of the year because they keep the cold and chills from your knees without making your legs too hot.

Race Cape

A race cape is simply a very lightweight waterproof jacket designed for cyclists. It's an invaluable item of clothing that offers the distinct advantage that it will scrunch up to fit easily into one of your jersey's pockets. Not only will a race cape keep you dry when it rains, it'll stave off spray from wet roads and also provide you with a windproof shell for those chilly mornings. When choosing a race cape, be aware that there are three items of clothing that superficially appear the same. The first is a jacket that is simply windproof - cheap, but of no use in wet conditions. The second is a showerproof jacket, which offers some wet weather protection and is cheaper than a full waterproof. Finally, there's the fully waterproof race cape, which, if it is of good quality, will be breathable too allowing you to avoid a boil-in-the-bag experience. If you can afford it, always buy a fully waterproof version.

Gilet

Similar to a race cape, a gilet offers protection from wind and moisture. Where it varies from a race cape is that it has no arms and is generally not fully waterproof - the lack of arms makes a fully waterproof garment a little redundant. Initially, considering the nature of race capes, it may seem that a gilet is an additional luxury. However, being lighter and covering only your torso, a gilet offers an excellent choice when it's a little chilly or you need to keep the cold of your chest during a long descent.

Shoe Covers

Having made a substantial investment in a lovely pair of shoes, you'll want to keep them in pristine condition. Alas, wet roads throw all sorts of debris up onto your shoes and they will suffer as a result. Also, wind and cold conditions can soon make your feet numb, and frozen feet are not fun when pedalling. A shoe cover is, as its name implies, a cover than encases your shoe. You slip the cover over your shoe - a little like putting on a sock. Although there are many shoe-covers on the market, they tend to fall into three categories:

1. Very lightweight and windproof.
2. Lightweight and waterproof.
3. Thick, waterproof and warm - typically a neoprene material.

Whichever you choose, remember to take your time rolling them onto your shoes and avoid forcing their progress - the zips or closures that secure them are prone to break with excessive force.

Long Gloves

Mitts are great in summer and fair conditions, but if you plan to ride out in all weathers, you'll need something more substantial. There's a huge range of long fingered gloves available varying in: style, level of warmth provided and fabrication material. If you just want to keep the chill off your fingers, choose what are in effect, long fingered mitts that are tactile with plenty of shock absorption for your hands. If on the other hand, you want to ride during really cold conditions, you'll need to choose something with far more insulation and that utilises a waterproof fabric. Whatever you choose, always make sure that you try them for fit and ease of removal - remember hands that are sweaty can make hard work when trying to remove a cheaper saturated glove.

Base Layers

A base layer looks like either a snug fit technical t-shirt or an elaborate string vest. If you watch professional cycle racing, you'll notice that regardless of the weather the riders often wear base layers under their jerseys. The reason for this is that a good base layer will wick moisture away from your body avoiding unnecessary chilling, keeping you cool when it's warm and conversely, keeping you warmer when the conditions are a little chilly.

What Not to Wear

From an early age, Italians learn that before they learn to ride well, they need to know how to look good. Any experienced rider will never fail to be shocked and amazed...even horrified, by some of the clothing crimes that people commit when rolling out for their weekend ride. The following list is not exhaustive, but it will prevent you from making a terrible faux pas and give you endless joy when you start looking out for these crimes of the road.

1. Mountain bike gear - wearing baggy shorts, chunky shoes and a full-face helmet is an absolute no no - unless of course you are mountain biking, or so fast that you feel the need to humiliate middle aged men in Lycra as you whizz past them.

2. Mismatched kit - as time advances, your collection of jerseys, shorts and mitts grows. You may fall into the trap of becoming lax and donning the first shorts and jersey that come to hand. Stop. Some clothing combinations are offensive to the eye, maybe, just maybe, they can cause accidents as other cyclist convulse from the sight of them. Do the world a courtesy and always check your attire before you roll.

Figure 20 The author commits crimes against cycling fashion

3. Hipster gear - no socks, rolled up jeans and no helmet may have their place in the confines of the world's trendier cities, but they have no place on the open road.

4. No socks - as previously mentioned, no socks mark you out as a triathlete and someone that has very smelly shoes. Socks were made for a reason - wear them.

5. Cycling tops with no sleeves - sticking with the triathlete theme, why do they all insist on jerseys with no sleeves? One can only assume it is to show off their mega muscles from all that swimming.

6. Aero helmets at the weekend - the time triallist may wear an aerodynamic helmet (solid and cone shaped) to cheat the wind and gain precious seconds when competing. However, wearing one outside of an event automatically lets everyone know to stay away - Class A nerd with no friends warning.

7. White shorts - see the Shorts section of this chapter.

8. Jumpers, coats and the like - you are not catching a train, taking a stroll in the autumn air or popping out for a romantic candlelight dinner, So there is no need whatsoever to wear civilian clothing...period.

9. The rucksack - for years, cyclists have hauled necessary spares, tools, clothing, food and drink with them by simply using a tiny saddle bag, their pockets and water bottle cages. If you need more storage than this, you need to reassess what you're taking with you - do you really need a Thermos?

10. Compression socks - some believe that compression socks offer a number of physiological benefits to the runner or cyclist. That's irrelevant, have any of these people seen what they look like? They're a disgrace with their overgrown hybrid socks. They really need to keep that sort of thing private and indoors.

Rounding Up

In this chapter, you've not only learnt about the essential clothing that every road rider needs, but you've also learnt about some of the more specialised clothing that will ensure that your rides are comfortable and that you always look the part. Of course, and perhaps most importantly, you've learnt what not to wear, avoiding some of cycling's worst faux pas.

Taking Your First Pedal Strokes

Figure 21 Practicing clipping in

Congratulations, you've bought a road bike and are standing on the side of the road dressed appropriately and ready to ride. So, what's next? Surely, you just turn the pedals and off you go? Well, yes - turning the pedals is a good idea but there are some things that can make road riding far easier and safer. In this chapter, we'll look at these things and discover how you can progress from someone who rode a bike as a kid to a real road rider.

> ## "Ride as much or as little, or as long or as short as you feel. But ride."
>
> Eddy Merckx

First Ride

Before you make that first turn of the pedals, did you buy a clipless pedal system as suggested in the Shoes section of the "Selecting the Right Gear" chapter? Yes, cool! Have you practiced clipping in and out? If not, roll your bike back home and find a solid surface (or willing helper) to offer some safety and support as you practice - Figure 21. It's all pretty simple: toe down, slide and listen for the click - you're in. Now, twist your heel out in a horizontal plane and, voila, you're free. Easy. You'll find that you'll always place one foot on the pedal first (90% of people use their right) - always clip this foot in first and out last. Finally, remember that when you're out on the road, you'll need to take a couple of pedal strokes before you clip in with your second foot so that you have some momentum and don't fall over.

> **Good to Know:** Some brands of pedal, such as Shimano and Speedplay, have adjustable spring tension. Reducing spring tension makes it easier for you to clip your foot in and out.

Good to Know: Always unclip one foot as you approach traffic hazards where you may have to stop. You'll still be able to pedal by resting your foot on the pedal, but most importantly, if you need to pop a foot to the ground you'll be ready. Remember, that once you have come to a complete standstill, you cannot unclip - gravity will win!

Good to Know: Sometimes your shoe has a life of its own and doesn't want to clip into the pedal. It's always tempting to look down at the pedal and shoe struggle. What are you doing? You can't see the bottom of your foot, but you'll certainly increase your chances of having an accident. Relax, take a few pedal strokes, and then try again.

Back to the roadside and it's time to start riding. Start pedalling and take your time, notice how the bike feels? Pretty fast and reactive, right? Now, get to grips with those shifters; try changing gears (both front and rear) and notice how it feels and how sometimes, you miss shift (no change, crunchy change, etc.). Happy? Time to test those brakes. Remember, they're sharp unlike the bikes that you may remember from childhood. Squeeze the brakes gently and at the same time, feel the sensation and how little effort you need to stop. Play with your bike for an hour or so. There's no rush, just get to feel how it reacts to your inputs.

Good to Know: It's important to use both brakes at the same time to maintain controlled braking. If you're too hard on the front brake, the front wheel may skid or you might catapult yourself over the handlebar! Equally, if you're too hard on the rear brake, you will make the rear wheel skid, which is not good for control or the life of your rear tyre.

> **Good to Know:** In countries where people drive and ride on the left-hand side of the road, the right-hand brake lever controls the front brake. Conversely, in countries where you ride on the right-hand side of the road, the left-hand lever controls the front brake.

Position

Hopefully, you took note of the "Getting the Right Fit" chapter, and you are sitting pretty and feeling good on your bike. Even with the correct size bike and a good fit, there are lots of people who seem to be glued in one position on their bikes. They're making a big mistake because a road bike with its drop handlebar is designed to allow the rider to adopt different positions depending on the terrain and desired riding result. In this section, we'll explore the different handlebar positions and how to use them like a pro.

The drop handlebar offers three primary positions and a number of less conventional positions. The primary positions are:

- On the Hoods.
- On the Tops.
- On the Drops.

In the following sections you will discover how and why you ride in these positions.

On the Hoods

This is the road rider's number one position and most riders spend the majority of their time in it. As Figure 22 shows, the rider's upper body is relaxed, a little upright while still in a somewhat aerodynamic position allowing the rider to cheat the wind. Not only is this position comfortable, it also allows you

Figure 22 Riding on the hoods

Figure 23 Riding on the drops

access to both the gears and the brakes without your hands moving position or leaving the handlebar.

On the Drops

This is the classic position that many people associate with road cycling. As Figure 23 shows, the rider is in a more prone position and their torso is closer to horizontal than when riding on the hoods. This position performs two key tasks. The first is that it drops the rider's centre of gravity. A lower centre of gravity equates to more stability and security when descending. Also, when descending, it is a great position because you only have to give the brakes the smallest of squeezes to utilise their power because you are using the full length of the brake lever. The second task is that because the rider's torso is closer to horizontal, they become far more aerodynamic. If you need to ride hard and fast, or cheat a nasty headwind, this position is for you.

> **Good to Know:** People with small hands sometimes struggle to use the brakes when riding on the drops. If this problem affects you, there are two solutions:
>
> 1. Change your bike's handlebar to one that has a shallower drop and smaller reach. This will move your hands closer to the brake levers and make the handlebar more comfortable. Any good bike shop will advise you on choosing a suitable size.
>
> 2. Some models of brakes allow for the insertion of shims in the brake levers, which bring the brake lever back closer to the handlebar. These shims, although effective, do limit the range that the brake levers can move, so are better adopted if a change of handlebar is not sufficient.

Putting aside descending and cheating the wind, riding on the drops offers an additional bonus: it's a great position for sprinting. Although you may not be about to enter any races, being able to sprint is a fundamental skill. Perhaps you're riding

Figure 24 Riding on the tops

Figure 25 Riding on top of the hoods

with a group that like to sprint for the town sign, or there's a wild-eyed farm dog chasing you down the road, either way a good sprint will help. The reason riding on the drops is good for sprinting is threefold. Firstly, the lower centre of gravity provides more stability. Secondly, as previously mentioned, you're more aerodynamic. Finally, the hand position provides stability through the use of the entire handlebar and it also allows you, in effect, to use the handlebar to leverage and propel the bike forward.

On the Tops

Sometimes, you'll feel the need to sit even more upright than when riding on the hoods - maybe you want to sit up and chat to a riding buddy or tap out a steady rhythm as you make a long climb. Riding on the tops achieves this and, as Figure 24 shows, the rider looks relaxed, upright and comfortable. This position is not only very comfortable, but it also opens up your chest allowing you to maximise your air intake. These are two of the main reasons why this is the most commonly adopted position for climbing.

> **Good to Know:** When climbing and riding on the tops, keep your fingers and hands relaxed - don't grip the handlebar. Visualise your fingers dangling like icicles. The reason for this is that relaxed hands translate to a relaxed upper body, which in turn means more of your energy is going to your legs and propelling you up the climb.

> **Good to Know:** Riding on the tops means that your hands are not next to the brake levers. Only ride in this position when there is no chance that you are going to need to brake suddenly.

That's the last of the primary positions and now that you've mastered these, there are some great additional positions you

Figure 26 Riding hugging the stem

Figure 27 Riding time trial style

can learn. Some of these will give your body a rest from being in one position for an extended period, and others offer further benefits such as enhanced aerodynamics. Some of the most common positions are:

On Top of the Hoods

This position is really a variant of the classic riding on the hoods position. The difference is that your hands curl around the very top of the ergo levers – as Figure 25 shows. The main benefit of this position is that it gives your body a rest from being in one position, it also elevates your head and torso slightly. Watch any long cycle race and you'll see riders in this position, you'll also notice that they often appear to be 'in the zone'. It's a focused cruising position.

Hugging the Stem

This is a fantastic position but is only suitable for experienced riders with good stability. As Figure 26 shows, the rider's hands are very close together - hugging the stem. The beauty of this position is that it puts you in a very comfortable upright position while, at the same time, narrowing your upper body making you much more aerodynamic than in many other positions. The bad news is that there are two serious downsides to this position. The first is that your hands are nowhere near the controls, which means you can't brake or change gear easily. The second is that you are steering the bike with, in effect, a nine-inch handlebar. The result of this is that the bike becomes incredibly twitchy and reactive to the slightest movement. Sudden or heavy-handed movements will send your bike into a nasty wobble that can easily end in a humiliating crash!

Time Trial Style

This position is provided for completeness and reference. It is incredibly dangerous and attempted by anyone other than a very experienced rider is very likely to result in a nasty crash. You have been warned - don't be tempted. It's included here because you will see it sooner or later if you watch cycle racing, especially where races include long descents, such as those found in the Alps or Pyrenees.

Figure 27 shows how the rider rests their forearms on the handlebar and adopts an almost prone praying position. By lowering their torso and narrowing their entire body, the rider becomes very aerodynamic and will achieve greater speeds on the flat and when descending. What the rider is doing is copying the position that they adopt on a time trial bike, which has a handlebar (known as an aero-bar) that specifically allows the rider to be in this position and still use all of the bikes controls. Of course, when they do this on a standard road bike, they have no access to the handlebar and no means of steering other than body weight and their forearms.

Pedalling

Now that you're more familiar with your bike, it's time to go for a proper ride. As you start riding, you'll soon settle into a rhythm and you'll feel the effort of climbing and the feeling of freedom as you descend. Now, you'll discover how your pedalling can become less taxing by adopting a few simple techniques.

Cadence

The number of times your legs make a complete revolution of the cranks and pedals per minute is your cadence. If your cadence is too low, your muscles will tire quickly or you'll be moving very slowly. On the other hand, if your cadence is too high, you'll use a lot of effort without moving very far – just like a hamster on its wheel. Back in the past, when people first started riding road bikes, their cadence was determined by the gearing of their bike – they only had one gear so their pedalling matched the terrain. With the advent of gears, riders could change gear so that they could maintain a consistent cadence regardless of whether the road was going up or down.

Some people may tell you that you should ride at a high cadence (90-100 rpm) and this may be right. However, this style was popularised by Lance Armstrong who adopted the technique to compensate for his reduction in muscle mass after cancer treatment. It's worth remembering that he also had an extremely high aerobic capacity and was able to utilise his heart and lungs to push massive amounts of oxygen to his muscles – not everyone has this capacity! The correct cadence is personal and reflects an individual's muscle mass, aerobic capacity and level of fitness. As a general rule, you should aim for a cadence of between 80 and 90 rpm. Experiment. If it's too fast or slow for you, adjust it until you find a rate with which you are comfortable. However, if that rate is outside of 70 to 100 rpm, you're very unlikely to be cycling efficiently and you may be more prone to physiological problems such as knee damage.

> **Good to Know:** Many cyclists find a cadence that is around 10 rpm slower than their usual rate works best when climbing. Try it and see if it works for you.

Perfect Circles

When you have the opportunity, watch how different riders pedal. Some have a fluid, effortless pedal stroke. Others have their legs pumping up and down like pistons and there are some that have a very ragged pedal stroke – almost as if they are pedalling in a square motion. How you pedal can have a huge impact on efficiency, power and endurance. A good pedal stroke is circular, which, of course, makes sense as cranks rotate in a circle around the bottom bracket. There have been numerous studies of the biomechanics of pedalling. Many of these focus on ankling – how the rider's ankle moves the foot during the pedal stroke. This level of detail, although important in the field of sports science, is hard to transfer to the bike whilst riding. There are, however, a number of tactics you can adopt to improve your pedal stroke:

1. Mindfulness – when pedalling, really focus on your stroke. Sense and feel how your joints move, the position of your feet and the sensation of the stroke that you are making. Aim to create a smooth circular motion.

2. Barrels – whilst pedalling, imagine you are standing on a barrel floating in calm water. Move the barrel underfoot to make it rotate – this creates the motion you are looking for. Couple this technique with mindfulness to achieve better results.

3. Off road – if you have the opportunity to cycle off road, whether on a mountain bike, hybrid or cyclocross bike, take it. Loose steep climbs require good pedalling and positioning on the bike to avoid the rear wheel slipping and spinning out from underneath the rider. This is one of the reasons that studies have shown that mountain bikers make some of the best climbers.

4. Spinning – pedalling at a very high cadence quickly highlights poor form through a ragged pedal stroke. During a descent or when you have a good tail wind, select an easy gear and pedal at the fastest cadence you can manage for one to two minutes. If you make this a regular part of your training rides, you'll notice that your maximum cadence and the fluidity of your pedal stroke will both improve.

5. Fixed wheel (a 'fixie') – a fixed wheel bike has no gears or freewheel, which means that the rider must pedal constantly. If you have the opportunity to ride a fixed wheel bike, you'll find that it highlights problems within your pedal stroke and it will help improve your fluidity.

Road Sense

Although you may have driven a car for a number of years, there's a big difference between driving and being a cyclist. For a start, you're much smaller, less visible and more vulnerable on a bike. Crucially, when cycling, an accident with other traffic can result in serious injury or death. Smart riding can greatly reduce your chances of becoming another grim statistic.

The Rider

Starting with you and your bike, make sure you're wearing a helmet and are visible to other road users. The traditional attire for UK road cyclists is black, but this is obviously not a wise choice in terms of visibility. Wear bright colours and if lighting conditions are poor, such as first thing in the morning, during early evening, or when the weather is poor, consider wearing some item of high visibility. For those that ride at night, high viz bands that wrap around an arm or leg are an excellent choice. Anything reflective on your legs will be highly visible to other road users because the human eye is automatically drawn to motion.

The Bike

If you're riding in the dark or poor visibility make sure that you have lights fitted to your bike. Bright rear lights are cheap and most are now USB rechargeable so you don't have to worry about the batteries wearing out. Front lights vary drastically in price depending on their power. Low power lights are cheap, and these will help make you visible to other road users, they will not, however, light the road in front of you. To see the road ahead, you'll need a light that produces an output of 500 lumens or more. A lumen is a measure of the total amount of light emitted by a light source – the greater the number, the more light that is produced.

Although it may seem obvious, ensure that your bike is road worthy. Tyres should be in good condition and correctly inflated, steering smooth and operational and both brakes in good working order. An alarming number of accidents occur when cyclists are unable to avoid a hazard or stop before an impact because their bikes are in poor condition. In 2017, there was a headline case in the UK where a cyclist riding a bike with no brakes, collided with and killed a pedestrian – the cyclist was jailed.

Weather

Modern cars with their ABS and traction control disconnect drivers from the road and they become unaware of how wet road surfaces can affect the handling of their cars. When you only have 23 mm of rubber connecting you to the road, you'll become very aware of wet road surfaces. Wet roads are slippery especially after periods of hot weather. Reduce your speed well in advance of corners and remember that your braking time will be much greater than in the dry. Also, pay special attention to painted road markings and any road furniture, such as manhole covers, gullies or rail lines. All of these can become exceptionally slippery when wet, resulting in ice-like conditions.

> **Good to Know:** It can be tempting to ride through puddles and see the water spray from your tyres. However much fun this might seem, puddles can hide potholes and other road hazards. Always approach puddles and flooded sections of road with extreme caution and, if you can, avoid them.

Road cycling is an addictive sport. You'll soon be so hooked that you'll want to ride regardless of the weather conditions. In some parts of the world, you simply must accept that rain is one of those things which you have to contend with. However, there are other weather conditions that require you to take extra care. In very hot areas, tar can become liquid and pool on corners, watch out for it. Conversely, snow and ice can linger after a thaw and both are incredibly dangerous on a road bike. It's best to sit it out and leave the bike at home on days like this – much better to ride another day than spend months recovering from a broken hip. Finally, be aware of high winds that can blow debris onto the road and also push you into oncoming traffic.

Defensive

Defensive riding is all about being seen, acting in advance and taking your place confidently on the road. Never ride in the gutter along the outside edge of the road. If you have to swerve to avoid debris or a pothole, you'll have nowhere to go but directly into the flow of traffic. Also, you'll pick up a lot more punctures riding through the debris and waste that collects alongside the road. If you can travel at the same speed as other traffic, it's usually best to place yourself in the centre of the flow of traffic. If, on the other hand, you are travelling at a slower pace than the other traffic, it is safer and more courteous to ride about one metre from the road edge.

When approaching junctions, move out either into the flow of traffic or, if the traffic is faster moving, a little further from the edge than you normally ride. This will help ensure that vehicles behind you won't try and squeeze past and then turn in front of you, and that you'll also be seen by vehicles that are waiting in adjoining roads. At traffic lights, stop junctions or roundabouts, take the centre of your lane, almost as if you were a car. At this point, all traffic is moving slowly so you're not an annoyance and you're in a position where other vehicles are unlikely to turn and hit you.

Rules

Most people will have seen cyclists jumping red lights, riding on pavements or going down one-way streets the wrong way. Not only does this kind of behaviour give all cyclists a bad name, but it also makes them more vulnerable to collisions. In most countries, all traffic laws and regulations apply to cyclists and additional guidance or legislation may also apply. Obey local traffic laws and regulations, it's better for you and better for all cyclists.

Figure 28 Beware of traffic hazards

Road Rage

Some people don't like cyclists – that's their problem. If you are abused by another road user, don't respond and just continue on your way. If they persist, take note of their registration and if you feel threatened, call the police. Responding to road rage is unlikely to achieve anything positive and you must remember that on a bike, you're in a very vulnerable position.

On the other hand, maybe you're the one feeling hot-headed. Perhaps a motorist cut you up or overtook you dangerously. Again, let it go - you'll achieve nothing other than to put yourself in danger. If you feel that someone else's behaviour was dangerous or truly unacceptable, note their registration and report them to the authorities.

> **Good to Know:** In many countries, including the UK, it is legal to ride two abreast. However, it's worth noting that if you are riding in the USA, you should check local traffic laws as individual states have differing rules. Before you choose to ride two abreast, it's courteous to consider whether you'll impede other road users.

Rounding Up

In this chapter, you have learnt how to clip in and out, the positions you can adopt on the bike and hopefully, have actually got out there and ridden. You then discovered how to maximise efficiency and performance through a good pedal stroke. Finally, you explored how to ride safely regardless of weather or traffic conditions. Well done, you're well on your way to becoming a road rider.

Getting More from Your Ride

Now that you've taken your first pedal strokes, it's time to explore some further areas that will improve your riding performance and enjoyment. In this chapter, you'll learn how training with heart rate monitoring and looking after your nutrition will take your riding to the next level.

> "Give a man a fish and feed him for a day.
> Teach a man to fish and feed him for a lifetime.
> Teach a man to cycle and he will realise
> fishing is stupid and boring."
>
> Desmond Tutu

Heart Rate and Training Zones

As in most sports, cyclists train to improve their speed and endurance. Any form of training requires measurement of progress so that the trainee can track their progress and adapt future training based on past performance. There are many forms of measurement ranging from how much a cyclist can leg press in the gym through to how long they take to complete a given ride. This said, the three main measures cyclists employ are:

1. Distance, time and feel – a simple cycle computer informs a rider of the distance they have covered, a watch provides the time ridden and the mind lets the rider know how they feel. These simple metrics are useful to record and fun to look back on as you track your progress. However, they are affected by external conditions such as weather, and they offer little precision when measuring effort.

2. Heart rate – heart rate increases with effort regardless of weather or terrain. Riding and training using heart rate data provides a simple method of gauging effort and fitness, which is more accurate than simply gauging effort through feel.

3. Power – power is a measure of how many watts of energy a cyclist produces whilst riding. The higher the wattage, the more power produced. For example, during a club ride someone may average 200 watts, whereas during a sprint that output may rise to 900 watts. Unlike heart rate, power measurements immediately reflect any change in the rider's effort and are not affected by natural variances in an individual's heart rate. Unfortunately, measuring power requires expensive equipment with entry level power meters starting at £600.

Because heart rate as a measure is both simple and affordable, in this chapter you'll discover how you can use it to improve your riding whether it's to speed recovery or to climb faster.

Heart Rate Monitors

Although not essential to your riding, a heart rate monitor (HRM) will allow you to learn quickly and easily what your heart and body are doing during exercise. As you become more experienced, you may choose to ride just on feel, or invest in a power meter that provides accurate feedback on how much power you are producing and pushing through the bike. For now, a HRM is a cheap investment that will improve your riding almost immediately. They start at around £20 and go upwards depending on the type and features available. Common styles include:

- Wrist mounted - watch style HRMs are available with two main types of sensor: the first sits in the back of the watch and measures heart rate through analysing light refracted off flowing blood. Although generally cheap, their results can sometimes be inaccurate. The second utilises a belt that straps around your chest. This system produces more accurate results.

- Cycle computer - a cycle computer provides the cyclist with lots of information through a display mounted on the handlebar or stem. Simple computers offer little more than distance and speed information, whereas more complex ones can provide GPS navigation and tracking. Many computers offer heart rate monitoring and, having the data displayed in front of you, is easier and safer than looking at a watch. Often, the HRM function is an option or requires the purchase of a separate chest belt - check carefully before you buy.

- An app - most cycle retailers sell brackets that allow you to mount your phone directly to your bike's handlebar or stem. Once you've done this, you can turn your phone into both a cycle computer and HRM. You'll need to install an app, such as Wahoo Cycling, and invest in some further hardware such as a HRM belt and sensors for your bike.

Maximum Heart Rate

To train and ride using heart rate monitoring, you'll first need to calculate your maximum heart rate. A laboratory can determine this quite accurately, but equally there are a couple of simple methods that you can use without specialised equipment. The first is the 220 minus your age technique, which is fairly accurate for the majority of people, but some will find that it is completely inaccurate for them. To use this method, simply subtract your age from 220 to establish your maximum heart rate, for example:

A 40-year-old:

220-40=180 Max Heart Rate

If this technique doesn't work for you, you can use a physical test which was proposed by *timetrialtraining.co.uk*. It is important to note that this test pushes your heart to its maximum, so you should only perform it when you are not tired or ill. Additionally, you should consult a doctor to ensure that you are fit and capable of performing such a test. The method: choose a short route that is primarily on flat roads or use a stationary trainer if you have one available. Warm up for fifteen minutes, so that you feel warm and perhaps have a slight sweat. Now ride as hard as you can for ten minutes at a consistent pace. Finally, go as fast and as hard as you can for the last 20 to 30 seconds. Check your heart rate – it is more or less at its maximum at this point. Drop down the gears and gently carry on cycling to warm down for a further ten to fifteen minutes. Ideally, you should perform this test a couple of times over a number of days to attain the most accurate result

Training Zones

Once you have determined your maximum heart rate, you can establish personal training zones to ensure that you get the most out of your riding. Each zone is based on a percentage of your maximum heart rate. Table 2 shows these zones together with actual heart rates based on a person with a maximum heart rate of 180 bpm.

So, what does all this mean for you? The majority of your rides should be in the Endurance and Aerobic zones. These rides will make you fitter, allow you to ride further and provide you with a solid foundation for future development. Threshold efforts, at this point, should be reserved for climbing and time trialling (see the "Moving Forward: Your Next Steps" chapter). As you become fitter, you'll spend more time working in this zone to improve your overall performance. The Max zone should be reserved for the occasional sprint – at this point, riding frequently in this zone is more likely to cause you problems than improve your riding. Finally, the Recovery zone provides an ideal place to ride after a hard effort, such as a big

Zone	Intensity	Purpose	% of Max HR	Example BPM
Recovery	Very easy. Soft pedalling and able to hold a conversation with ease.	Start warm ups and end cool downs in this zone. Active recovery after hard efforts.	50-60	90-108
Endurance	Easy and comfortable. Light gears. Able to hold a conversation with ease.	Improves endurance and allows you to ride for long periods.	60-70	108-126
Aerobic	Moderate effort. Able to talk in short sentences. Light sweating. Some resistance through the pedals.	Improves aerobic fitness.	70-80	126-144
Threshold	Hard. Difficult to speak at all – single words.	Improves max performance and speed.	80-90	144-162
Max	Very Hard. Can't speak.	Improves explosive speed and top-end performance. For very short periods only.	90-100	162-180

Table 2 Cycling heart rate zones

climb and as part of your warm up and cool down during each ride. Once you have developed a reasonable level of fitness, you can take short rides (30-40 mins) in the Recovery zone as active recovery rides – these will help you recover after a previous day's hard ride. It's interesting that many new riders fail to build enough recovery in to their training. Failing to recover, whether active or inactive, impacts your ability to improve performance over time and, in fact, may have a negative impact on your overall performance.

Lactic Threshold

Have you noticed that when you climb a hill you start to become breathless and your heart rate rises? Climbing hills is hard work and your heart is pumping faster to push oxygen to those all-important leg muscles. As your effort-level increases, so too does your muscles' need for oxygen. If you push hard whilst riding on the flat, you'll notice that exactly the same thing happens. If you've pushed really hard, you might experience a strange feeling where your legs feel as if they have turned to lead. Suddenly, you'll find that it's impossible to progress at the same pace and your legs will scream with pain. Unfortunately, as your muscles use all that lovely oxygen, they deposit a waste product called lactic acid. Luckily, your body can wash away this acid so that you can operate in a normal way. However, as the level of lactic acid mounts, it will reach a point where your body can simply no longer clear it faster than it is being produced. It is at this point, known as the lactic threshold, that your muscles scream and feel as though they have turned to lead.

It takes time to clear accumulated lactic acid from your body, so it makes sense to avoid crossing the lactic threshold. So, how do you know where your lactic threshold is? It varies from person to person, so there's no universal measurement. If you are willing to spend plenty of money, you could gain access to a sports science laboratory where they can take a blood sample and tell you your lactic threshold. Obviously, this isn't the simplest thing in the world and equally, a lactic threshold measurement won't actually have any practical use on the road. Instead, a much simpler solution is to perform a simple practical experiment that will give you a good indication of your lactic threshold expressed as a percentage of your maximum heart rate.

Find a long hill and climb whilst maintaining a steady heart rate. If you start to feel the lactic acid build up, you've gone over your threshold. On the other hand, if you feel fine, try pushing it a little harder next time. Once you find your personal sweet-spot where pushing any harder will take you in to the red, check your heart rate and this is approximately your lactate threshold. Whenever you're climbing or pushing hard, try to keep your heart rate at this level and you'll avoid going into the red, crossing your lactic threshold and causing premature exhaustion.

Hydration and Food

For rides lasting less than 90 minutes, nutrition and hydration are not major issues – fill a bottle with water and pop it into your bottle cage. However for longer rides, you must ensure that you have an adequate intake of calories and maintain the electrolytes in your body. In this section, we'll explore the basics of sports nutrition to help you ride longer and faster and recover effectively after rides.

If you think of your body as an engine, its fuel comes from two main sources: fat, and carbohydrate stored as glycogen in the liver and muscles. Your body can store a limited amount of glycogen and this varies between individuals but is generally adequate for 90 minutes of riding. All cycling burns a mixture of carbohydrate and fat, but as the intensity increases the percentage coming from carbohydrate increases and conversely, the percentage from fat decreases – see Figure 29. You don't need to worry about running out of energy deriving from fat because even the most trained athletes have fat stores that far exceed the amount they could possibly burn during activity. On the other hand, running out of glycogen is a real threat to cyclists and may resulting in 'bonking' – a term given to when you feel total fatigue and a complete loss of energy. Correct fuelling before and during a ride will ensure that you don't experience this unpleasant sensation.

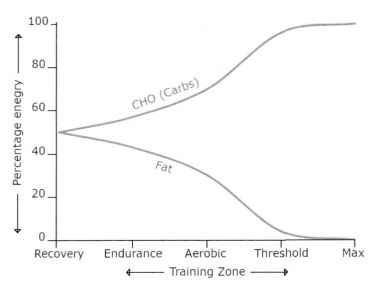

Figure 29 Carbohydrate vs fat

Pre-ride Fuelling

Eating well before a ride ensures that you top up your glycogen stores and have sufficient fuel for your muscles. If you plan on taking a long ride, you need to start your nutritional preparation the day before. Ensure that you remain well hydrated – it's too late when you start riding. The evening before your ride, it helps to top up your glycogen stores and to avoid food that may upset your stomach. A meal rich in complex carbohydrates and lean protein sources will give your body the best start. For example, brown rice with chicken breast or quinoa with salmon.

> **Good to Know:** Keeping hydrated is important, but equally drinking too much can cause serious problems. Excessive consumption of water can dilute the salts within your body and cause excess liquid to form around the brain and kidneys. Taken to the extreme, excess fluid can result in serious problems or even death. According to the research of Christopher McDougal, author of Born to Run, there is no documented case of anyone dying during a marathon due to insufficient fluid, but there are several documented cases of fatalities due to excess fluid intake.

The morning of your ride, you must start with a good breakfast an hour or two before you depart. If your planned ride is two to three hours, a breakfast rich in complex carbohydrates, such as porridge, is ideal. It'll top up your glycogen stores and slowly release its energy as you ride. If, on the other hand you plan on a long ride, adding a source of lean protein to your meal increases endurance. Eggs provide an easy way to boost protein, but scrambled tofu or a quinoa porridge will also do the trick. Whatever you choose to eat, ensure that you are well hydrated and avoid excessive quantities of caffeine, which as a diuretic, will reduce your hydration.

Nutrition on the Bike

Even experienced cyclists fail to fuel properly when on the bike and this can result in a loss of power and endurance capacity. The key to good fuelling is to start early and eat frequently. Ideally, you should start eating small amounts twenty minutes into your ride and continue eating every twenty minutes throughout the ride. This approach does not overwhelm your stomach and ensures that you keep your energy levels high.

During your ride you need to eat simple carbohydrates that enter your bloodstream quickly. There are numerous commercial sports nutrition products available and these provide everything that you need to keep adequately fuelled. Table 3 shows the main types of products. Alternatively, you can choose traditional foods, such as bananas and dried fruit.

Product	Description
Bars	Energy bars are easy to eat on the move and most provide a mixture of carbohydrates and protein, making them ideal fuel for longer rides. They come in several flavours to suit your taste and to avoid food boredom. When choosing bars, be careful not to select protein bars which are designed for recovery rather than immediate fuelling.
Gels	Energy gels are a suspension of carbohydrates in liquid. They are easy to consume whilst riding and ideal if you find it hard to stomach solid fuel when exercising. There are numerous flavours available and you'll see that some are caffeinated. Caffeine can aid performance and also provide a pick-me-up if you're tired – just don't overdo it!
Blocks	Gel blocks provide carbohydrate in a simple to eat format that can help alleviate food boredom. Like gels, some versions are caffeinated.
Beans	Very similar to jelly beans, these energy beans provide an easy to eat snack that helps mix up your food intake.
Drinks	There are numerous sports drinks available, these normally come either in a powder or tabular format – simply add them to water. Some drinks provide carbohydrate only (for short to medium rides), some provide carbohydrate and electrolytes (for longer rides) and others provide electrolytes with no carbohydrate (if you choose food as your energy source or for short rides).

Table 3 Sports nutrition products

Most sports nutrition companies recommend 60 – 90 grams of carbohydrate per hour for keeping your body fuelled. This carbohydrate can come from a mixture of food and drink. All nutrition products will display how much carbohydrate they provide and you'll find that most manufacturers label their products as units or servings, where each unit provides 30 grams of carbohydrate. Typically, a product will contain 30 or 60 grams of carbohydrate. For example, gels normally contain 30 grams of carbohydrate and larger bars 60 grams. Therefore, if you're drinking plain water and consuming half a bar and two gels during an hour's cycling, you will take in 90 grams of carbohydrate.

Figure 30 Keeping fuelled

Getting your carbohydrate from a mixture of food and drink sources is a good idea. You will find that during longer rides, you will become bored of eating the same food repeatedly. Also, further into a long ride or during lengthy climbs, you may find it hard to eat solid food so having some gels will provide a welcome change. Generally, a long ride's fuelling will start with bars then move onto gels, whilst gaining carbohydrate throughout the entire ride through drinks.

Good to Know: There's a growing school of thought that turns the idea of performance diets on their head and spurns carbohydrate rich diets. These diets relate to all the food and drink that an athlete consumes whether on or off the bike. Such approaches require the body to go through a period of adaption to reduce the body's need for sugar rich simple carbohydrates. If you want to experiment with such an approach, there's a wide range of reputable research with which you should become acquainted to avoid health or performance problems.

Post-ride Fuelling

If you've had a long or hard ride, you'll need to refuel post-ride to get ready for your next ride and to help your body repair itself. Protein will help repair damaged muscles and you should get this from sources such as chicken breast, eggs or lentils. You also need to add some good quality carbohydrate to top up your glycogen stores. Avoid sugary foods and drinks, and instead opt for whole grains and vegetables. Finally, ensure that you're hydrated – it's easy to become dehydrated when cycling despite your best efforts. As a rule of thumb, if your urine is not clear or light coloured, you're lacking in fluids. If you do need to top up your fluids, take small quantities of fluid on a regular basis rather than drink a large quantity in one go.

Rounding Up

In this chapter, you've learnt about lactic acid and how this affects your riding as well as how you can establish your lactic threshold. You then discovered how you can use your heart rate to train and improve performance and endurance. Finally, you explored nutrition and hydration so that you can keep your body well fuelled before, during and after a ride.

Climbing:
The Ugly Truth

Many would say that climbing is both the hardest and most rewarding aspect of road cycling. Done badly, it offers little more than a solitary world of suffering. On the other hand, if you get it right, you are liberated and soar past people as you float like an eagle ever upwards towards the reward of your climb's summit. In this chapter, you'll start with basics and progress to climbing like a pro - admittedly, at a somewhat slower pace!

"The mountains are the pinnacle of suffering."

Greg LeMond

Types of Climbs

Technically, if the road rises past horizontal and points upwards, you're climbing. At the easiest in terms of steepness, there are false flats which have a gradient below two percent, and which, although when riding them you are gaining height, cyclists don't describe them as a climb. In fact, they'll use almost any verb to describe movement on a false flat: crawling, smashing, chewing up, spitting out, mashing, destroying, crushing, etc. The false flat may not register as a climb, but be warned that it can tire your legs and often marks the start of a serious climb. You'll know that you've moved beyond a false flat and are actually climbing once the gradient rises above two percent.

The French say that wine is an expression of its terroir. It's every element of a vine's environment that goes into the flavour of the grapes, not simply a generic taste associated with a grape variety. And so it is with climbs. They vary in length, steepness, profile, road surface and environment. All of these things combine to give every climb its unique signature. Not only does each climb have a unique signature, each will be different on any given day or even time of day – climbing possibilities are endless.

Figure 31 Sa Calobra, Mallorca

Really, there's no technical distinction that separates different climbs, but it will help you later in this chapter if you think of four main types:

1. Short and punchy.
2. Rollers.
3. Long hills.
4. Mountains.

Short punchy climbs are less than half a mile in length but often much shorter, and they're characterised by steep gradients, typically 15% to 33%. These are the type of hills that scream for a rider to attack them, to conquer them as quickly as possible.

Rollers are longer hills often found in a series as you ride along a road. The gradients are generally not that steep (4% to 8%), the length not too long (maybe up to a mile), but you'll still need to work. You'll know a roller opposed to a long hill because it'll never have a name, they are the anonymous hills of the cycling world.

A long hill is similar to a roller, but it may be steeper in places, it'll be longer - maybe a mile to five miles in length - and it'll have a name. Most areas will have long hills that local riders always include in their rides and of which they can recount various stories of battles and events that have taken place.

Mountains are an entirely different world. They're long, often in double figures of miles. Their gradients are sometimes consistent, but frequently fluctuate between small sections of descent ramping up to gradients found on short punchy climbs. All mountains are hard and take time to climb. They're the climbs where cycling shifts from being a physiological game to a mental game.

In the following sections, you'll learn how to conquer all of these types of climb using specific techniques for each type.

Physiology of Climbing

Take a look at the best climbers in the world and you'll make no significant connection between place of birth, height or sometimes even technique. What you will find is that they have alarming power to weight ratios, which means they are characterised by very low body fat and puny upper bodies. This is no coincidence. One of the greatest influences on the speed that a rider can climb is their power-to-weight ratio. The more power and the less weight, the greater the ratio and the faster the rider can propel themselves upwards. For example, every kilo saved whilst climbing the legendary Alp d'Huez results in a saving of 24 seconds.

This simple concept led riders of the past to drill holes in their bikes to reduce weight in an attempt to achieve an advantage. Today, people tend to leave the drill at home for DIY tasks, and instead, spend extravagantly to buy the lightest bike and wheels they can afford. Others prefer to lose some of their excess personal weight through training and diet, which has the potential to achieve the greatest impact on power to weight. Be warned though, if you are tempted to follow an extreme diet, you may lose valuable muscle as well as fat and may actually reduce your overall power!

Before you become totally obsessed with shaving weight off you and your bike, the following sections will provide you with an army of tools to help you nail those climbs – all with no additional cost.

Short Punchy

Short punchy climbs are difficult to climb seated because their gradients are so steep - you'll soon find that you run out of gears and painfully crawl along the final metres of the climb. Instead, you are better off attacking these climbs as shown in Figure 32.

If you're sure that the next climb is short and punchy, approach it in a medium gear with a good pedal cadence. As the climb starts to ramp, you'll feel your legs suddenly taking an additional load. Change down a gear or two and keep a solid pace. Once you start to slow below your previous cruising speed, you need to attack. Place your hands around the hoods and prepare to stand. As your cadence starts to drop, stand and allow your body weight to push the pedals round and let the bike gently shift from side to side under your upright body. You're not trying to thrash the bike up the hill, it's more that you are dancing your way upwards (the French say '*comme un danseur*'). One by one, shift through the gears whilst maintaining a balance between having adequate resistance through the pedals to becoming bogged down by the size of the gear. Your heart rate will jump and your breathing will deepen. Feel the love for this, but don't push yourself into the red. As you near the summit, drop down a gear, sit and power through the final metres. Once you've crested, keep your legs turning, easy pedal so that you feel little resistance through the pedals. Allow your body to recover. Glance back at the riders you've left in your wake!

Figure 32 Attacking a short climb

Rollers

For most people, rollers are horrible climbs. There's no real summit, no sense of achievement and you know there's another one not too far down the road. With a little knowledge you can tame these hills, conserving your energy for more important and notable climbs.

The key to riding rollers is to keep seated and to control your heart rate. As you approach the climb, drop down a gear and maintain a good cadence (say 90 rpm). Allow your breathing and heart rate to rise but stay within your tempo range (able to exchange very short sentences). Keep shifting as your cadence drops and concentrate on keeping everything steady and not over reaching yourself. Within a couple of minutes, you'll near the summit. Continue with the same effort and cadence, don't feel the need to push hard during the final metres. As you crest the summit, change up a gear and continue on your way. If you feel the need, soft pedal whilst keeping your legs spinning as you descend the other side. That said, it's a good idea to take advantage of the descent to set yourself up for the next roller by gathering speed so that you propel yourself up the start of the next climb – it's easier to gather speed going downhill than when climbing.

Long Hills

Long hills are fun – they're the place where you prove your ability during a weekend ride with friends. You know that you have to continue riding once the climb is done, but equally you don't mind pushing hard because there will be time to recover - hopefully on a great descent or with a coffee and cake stop.

If you're riding with a group and you're not a mountain goat, position yourself near the front of the group as you approach the climb. This means that although faster riders will pass you as they climb, you'll not be so far behind when you reach the summit. Then, approach the climb just as you would a roller: drop down a gear, stay seated and maintain your cadence. When riding with a group, a wave of excitement will always pass through the riders. The best climbers will disappear into the distance and the hopefuls will try to stay with them. Forget them all. The hopefuls will push too hard, go into the red and you'll soon pass them on your steady course to the top.

After a minute or so, your body will adjust to the climb and your heart rate and breathing will settle. You can push a little harder than when climbing a roller – you should be able to spit out single words such as 'OK' or 'good'. Find your pace and stick with it. Use your gears to maintain cadence and effort. You may find that your cadence drops a little - perhaps reducing to something more like 70 rpm. This is fine – everyone has their own climbing cadence. Just don't allow your legs to get bogged down in the gear. If you're fighting the gear, you will prematurely tire your muscles and you'll pay later during the climb.

Figure 33 Enjoying a long hill

Occasionally, the gradient will lessen. If you're tiring, use these sections to ease off just a little to allow your breathing and heart rate to recover. On the other hand, the gradient may sharpen – perhaps as you round a corner. If you feel the need to stand so that you can continue in the same gear, do so. Otherwise, if you prefer to remain seated, drop down a gear and maintain your cadence and effort. Remember that if you change gear in advance of the steep section, you'll avoid crunching the gears and losing momentum.

As you approach the summit, shift up a gear and push harder. You're not quite sprinting, but you're almost giving it everything that you've got. As you crest the summit, keep your legs turning – soft pedal. Sit up and let your breathing and heart rate regulate. Congratulate yourself and go to the cafe with a big smile on your face.

Mountains

Mountains are the ultimate test of a rider's climbing ability. Although in this section you'll learn about the physical aspects of climbing mountains, the following section "Psychology of Climbing" is more important. Climbing mountains is 80% mental and 20% physical. This comes in to play even more so because most riders will only tackle mountains whilst travelling abroad or to other parts of the country.

As you approach a mountain, all kinds of thoughts will fly around your head. You'll be wondering how hard can it really be? There may be a nagging doubt whether you'll make it to the top. Perhaps you'll have recollections of the last time you tackled this particular climb. Whatever you are thinking, the thoughts will soon pass as you take those first tentative pedal strokes on the climb's opening slopes. Some mountains ease you in with gentle inclines that gradually steepen; others present you with a seeming brick wall– Alp d'Huez springs to mind. However they start, you need to use the skills you have already developed to ensure that you stay riding within your physical means. As soon as you push your body into the red, you'll be on a downward spiral that ends in exhaustion and a never-ending slog upwards and onwards.

As you climb, change gear to keep your legs spinning and your heart rate and breathing under control. You need to be able to utter short sentences. If you can't, reduce your pace. As the minutes pass and you see your elevation rise, you'll move in to a steady climbing zone becoming more focused on your breathing and how the bike feels under your control. You become one with the bike and the mountain. Every so often, the road will change gradient. If it eases, take the opportunity to allow your body to recover by soft pedalling. If it increases, change down through the gears and keep your steady tempo. Don't be tempted to jump out of the saddle too often. Climbing out of the saddle requires more energy and any boost to speed will soon be lost.

> **Good to Know:** There's an old saying that goes, "Drink before you're thirsty, eat before you're hungry." This has never been so true as on a mountain. Sweating results in rapid fluid loss, which is proven to reduce performance and will ultimately impair your mental capacity – this is when accidents and hypothermia can inflict themselves.

Sat in the same position, working hard, you'll experience aches and pains: your hands become numb, a muscle throbs somewhere in your leg, your backside deadens or your neck and back begin to ache. This is normal. Change your position slightly to give your body some relief. Try switching hand positions or standing for a short distance. Try anything, but do not stop. Once you stop, your muscles quickly lose heat and once you restart, it won't be long until you ache even more or suffer cramps.

> **Good to Know:** When you ride in the mountains, your skin is subject to greater levels of UV than when at lower altitudes. So even though it may not feel so hot, splash on the sunscreen before each ride.

When you approach steeper sections of the climb, the road will often weave its way upwards through a series of hairpin bends. These bends become very steep on their inside and are always much slacker on their outside edge. Within the limits of safety, use all of the road available to you to avoid the steepest inclines. You can also use these changes of gradient to catapult you out of the bend. As you pass the apex of the bend, follow the diagonal line of least resistance back to the other side of the road (or lane). You will accelerate as you are, in effect, cycling across a slacker gradient than any part of the bend. This technique requires practice but once mastered, gives you a series of mini turbo boosts.

If a hairpin is particularly steep or you simply don't want to change down a gear, stand as you enter the bend and then as you cut back across the road, sit down and take advantage of the additional speed.

The immediate environment surrounding the climb can also affect the techniques you adopt. Look for areas of shade. Take advantage of these to allow your body to cool a little. Likewise, if there's been rain recently, perhaps a small shower and the road is wet, breathe deeply and take advantage of the additional oxygen in the air. Also, when looking at the road, watch out for smoother areas of tarmac that offer less resistance to your tyres. Survey your environment constantly as you progress and ask yourself whether you can take advantage of changes within it.

You are armed with a good selection of techniques that will allow you to conquer almost any mountain. That said, you will reach a point where your body is exhausted, you hurt and your morale is gone. It's at this point that any physical techniques offer little value – you have entered one of the hardest parts of climbing. As you will discover in the next section, you climb mountains with your mind not your legs.

Psychology of Climbing

It's an interesting thing that as a climb steepens and lengthens, the rider's techniques shift from those that are physical to those

Figure 34 Mountain climbing in Mallorca

that are mental or psychological. Short climbs often reflect the strength of a rider, whereas long climbs present the mind of the rider. In this section, you'll discover many of the techniques and methods that pro's and other great climbers adopt. You'll gain the mental armoury that will push your climbing to another level.

The Basics

You've duly noted all of the advice in the previous sections, jumped on your bike and climbed a few hills. It turns out that it wasn't that easy – seemed easy reading about it, right? Well, nothing's going to make climbing easy (perhaps going really slowly might?), but there are some basic mental techniques that will make it less agonising. To commence, in an absolute nutshell there are two fundamental rules to climbing.

The first is never stop...never, period! Stopping and even worse stopping and walking, affects both the body and mind. Your body will cool, your muscles may cramp and any respite will only be temporary. Mentally, stopping sets off an internal dialogue that says things like:

- "This climb is too hard for me".
- "I'm never going to make it".
- "I'm a rubbish climber".
- "I'm weak".
- "I won't make it to the top".

What makes things worse is that once you stop once, you are giving yourself permission to stop again in the future. It's a slippery slope. One where you will never be able to climb anything 'hard' without stopping, resting or walking. You will, simply put, never be able to climb. Stay on the bike and keep moving, it's the only way to progress.

The second rule is to sectionalise. Maybe a climb feels too long, too steep – it's just too big for you at this time. But how about just making it to the post a hundred metres up the road? That's going to be achievable, isn't it? As you close in on the post, shift your attention to the tree twenty metres further on. As you approach each marker, set another further up the climb. Slowly and surely you will crest what was once a seemingly unclimbable hill or mountain.

As you become more proficient as a climber, you can adopt a twist on this sectionalising approach: select moving targets. On busier climbs, improve your pace and keep your motivation high as you select riders in the distance as targets. Don't push too hard but keep the rider in sight, eventually catching and passing them. Now search for another.

> **Good to Know:** Although sectionalising is a very common dissociation technique, there are many others that people adopt including singing songs, admiring the view, performing mental arithmetic and counting pedal strokes. Regardless of how silly the technique might appear, if it works for you, use it.

Climbing with Others

You've learnt the basics of climbing and you've conquered a few climbs. Now you start riding with others, perhaps in a group. As you roll together, a climb approaches and a wave of anticipation passes amongst you. Some riders jostle for position and others appear to drop back – it's as if they have admitted defeat before they've even started.

Earlier, you learnt to position yourself near the front of the group to make up for any lack of climbing prowess. So you're well positioned and then the hammer drops – fellow riders launch themselves into the climb. Maybe you'll be dropped? Maybe others will gain an advantage as they push hard at the start of the climb? Ride within yourself and put aside the actions of others. You'll claw back any ground lost to those that started too hard, and those that are truly faster than you will be gone – don't get caught up trying to out climb the mountain goats. Remind yourself that this is your climb and you will make it within the best of your abilities.

There may be riders cranking their way up the climb that are within view, seemingly within reach. It would be nice to catch and pass them, for sure. Think tactically. If you push too hard, you'll blow up shortly after passing them. Increase your tempo slightly and glance towards them from time to time to assess your progress. If you're gaining, keep that tempo; if you're not, think whether pushing any harder will take you in to the red or whether you have a little more in the tank. To view this solid determined approach to climbing, take a look at some classic Tour de France footage. Riders such as Ulrich, Evans and frequently Froome all took the approach of steady progress. When riders such as Armstrong, Schleck and Contador attacked, they didn't automatically react. They knew that continuously reacting to spurts and attacks from other riders would wear them down and eventually push them into premature exhaustion.

"If it hurts me, it must hurt the others twice as much."

Jens Voigt

Alongside you, you may find another rider matches you pedal stroke by pedal stroke. It's almost like you're joined by an invisible thread. Remind yourself that they are hurting too. If you can, take a drink from your bottle. It will discourage the other rider – make them think that you have plenty of spare energy – attacking is pointless. Try to give nothing away: don't say how hard the climb is – keep a poker face. If the other rider senses weakness, they'll up the tempo or attack and that's

Figure 35 Sitting on the wheel

another rider who will finish in front of you. Likewise, if you see signs of weakness in your companion, don't attack – just up the tempo and slowly ride away from them. The chances are that they'll push hard to get back on your wheel. Up your tempo a little again. Soon, you'll be aware that the rider is yo-yoing: struggling to get back on your wheel and then repeatedly dropping back. Once this happens, you know they are beat – dig deep and persevere.

Sometimes, you'll sense a rider lingering just behind you – sat on your wheel as shown in Figure 35. They're using you to keep their pace and push themselves just that little bit harder. A cyclist on your wheel saps your physical and mental energy. Take the previous approach of upping the tempo and slowly ride away. If you don't drop the rider, consider moving out and back – perhaps feigning drinking from your bottle. Swap roles. Sit on their wheel and allow them to do the hard work. It's one of the innate facts of climbing: it's easier to follow a wheel than to ride alone.

Big Climbs

Big climbs require you to adopt a complete mental game plan. When you start climbing a mountain, you'll feel a mixture of anticipation, excitement and fear. Once you find your rhythm, things settle in your mind and you focus on breathing and pedalling. As the miles grind on and steeper sections present themselves, you'll start to feel pain and your mind will start to play games. You're sure that there's a problem with your bike - the tyres feel soft, the brakes are rubbing, the gears are just not quite right. And, yes, a little rest or check of your bike would be so good, wouldn't it? Or, maybe, just maybe, this would be a great spot to pull over and take a selfie, don't you think? It's all in your mind - your bike's fine and you look terrible, so a selfie isn't really the greatest idea. Your mind wants you to stop – to give in, give up. Don't!

Keeping going is the hardest element of climbing any mountain. Taken section by section, piece by piece, you can ride any part of this mountain. In combination, these sections create a challenge that is not only physically demanding, but mentally, seemingly unsurmountable. Remind yourself that you must keep going. Keep focused on your breathing, your cadence and your level of effort. Cast aside those niggles of self-doubt. When things get really tough, remind yourself of the basics. Sectionalise. Think next bend, next tree, next pebble on the roadside. Whatever it takes, break the climb up into fragments that you can manage. You will enter a solitary world. One that consists of you, your bike and the mountain. Be one in this world. It's a lonely place, but one that will eventually lead to the reward of standing at the summit knowing that you, and you alone, have conquered the climb.

"When my legs hurt, I say: 'Shut up legs! Do what I tell you to do!'"

Jens Voigt

Rounding Up

In this chapter, you've explored the different types of climbs and discovered the techniques to conquer them. Underlying these techniques were the two golden rules of climbing: sectionalise and never stop. As you progressed from local climbs to those in the mountains, you explored the psychology of climbing and how, in order to conquer mountains, you must win the mental game to stand aloft at the summit.

Descending: Trade Secrets

The reward for battling your way up a climb is the descent that awaits. A descent taken well is an art – you flow gracefully down the mountain, sweeping around each turn, fluidity identifies you as an expert descender. Yet, there are so many people who are gripped by fear – who slowly and painfully make their way down what should be a dream roller coaster ride. Fortunately, in this chapter you'll discover techniques and approaches that will enable you to descend like a pro.

"My biggest fear isn't crashing this bike at 85 mph and losing my skin - it's sitting in a chair at 90 and thinking 'I wish I'd done more'"

Graeme Obree

Basics of Position

As your front wheel points downwards and gravity takes over from your tired muscles, you start your descent. Shake out any tired limbs and then position yourself on the bike. The best position for descending is with your hands on the drops. In this position, your centre of gravity is lower and this makes the bike easier to control. If you don't feel comfortable on the drops, you should revisit the "Getting the Right Fit" chapter earlier in this book. You will see many people descending with their hands on the hoods. This is often because of a poorly fitted bike, or it could be that they want to sit up and take the descent easily whilst recovering from the preceding climb.

With your hands on the drops, ensure that you can throw out a finger to pull the brake lever. Because you are using the full length of the brake lever, one finger is all that you need to brake hard. It's a good idea to never use more than one finger because if you hit a bump or hole in the road, your hands can easily lose contact with the handlebar. Although you are holding the handlebar, make sure that your hands and arms are relaxed. Rigid or tense arms make it very difficult to steer and can lead to making sudden sharp moves, such as pulling the brakes too hard. Continue with the relaxation theme and allow your entire body to relax. If your body relaxes, it helps reduce anxiety and fear – you don't want to feel fear.

Figure 36 Relaxed whilst descending

Keep your legs moving – soft pedal or even just simply spin with no resistance. It can be tempting to sit up and coast along, but once you hit the flat or the next climb, your cold legs will feel like lead – they'll scream with pain! Keeping your legs moving allows the blood to continue to flow and the toxins and lactic acid that built up during the climb to clear. Most descents vary in gradient and often have small sections of flat or even short rises. If you use your gears to keep a little resistance, you'll be well positioned for when these changes take place.

Your hands may be on the drops, but you need to keep your head up with your eyes scanning the road ahead. As your speed increases, you need to look further and further down the road. You want to be able to spot hazards and bends in the roads well in advance so that you can take them in your flow rather than having to react at the last second. Your goal is to maintain a smooth, fluid line – think smooth arcs rather than choppy movements.

Taking corners

Anyone can go down a hill fast – ignore fear and common sense, and don't touch the brakes! Speed doesn't equate to a good descender. In fact, it is the ability to take corners well that highlights the riders with real skill. Corners taken well are beautiful, they give you a nice feeling of being one with the bike. On the other hand, corners taken badly can be scary and dangerous. In this section you'll discover some techniques that will allow you to corner with confidence, speed and finesse.

The basic approach for taking a corner involves combing three distinct aspects:

1. Line choice.
2. Braking.
3. Body position.

Possibly the most important rule to remember is to not brake in corners – you must scrub excess speed before you enter the bend. The reason for this is that a bike under braking will travel in a straight-line – it's simply a question of physics. If you're braking, you cannot turn – period! It takes a lot of practice to learn how fast you can take a given bend, so when you are learning, slow your speed so that you are travelling slower than you think you'll be able to take the bend. As you gain experience, you'll be able to corner faster. For the moment, focus on good form – speed will come with practice.

> **Good to Know:** Your bike follows your eyes. Your body, and therefore your bike, tend to go wherever you look. If you look at a pothole, you've a good chance of riding in to it. On the other hand, visualise a safe cornering line set out in front of you and this is the line that you'll follow.

Once you've reduced your speed, you need to consider the line that you'll take. Whenever you descend, you're striving to move in smooth fluid lines. The smoothest line will be the one that has the most relaxed angle and requires the least amount of movement to complete. Figure 37 illustrates this line. Notice that the rider goes from the outside of the bend to the inside (apex) of the bend, and then back to the outside of the bend. It doesn't matter if it's a left or right-handed bend, or whether it is on the flat or a steep descent – the line remains the same: outside-inside-outside.

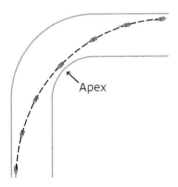

Figure 37 Cornering line

As you approach a corner, move smoothly to its outside edge. Before doing so, remember to assess road and traffic conditions. If the bend is blind or traffic is high, you don't want to position yourself too close to the centre of the road because doing so puts you in the line of oncoming traffic. Equally, be extremely cautious of using the entire width of the road – you are very exposed and probably causing a traffic offence.

Figure 38 Weight through outside foot

Now that you are in the correct starting position to take the bend, you need to position your body correctly. You already know that you should have your hands on the drops with relaxed torso and limbs. You now need to position your legs and feet. Your foot that's on the outside of the bend should be at the bottom of the pedal stroke (6 o'clock position) and your inner foot at the top of the pedal stroke (12 o'clock position) – see Figure 38. You may see some riders cornering with both feet level. This is normally because they have misunderstood advice on descending – don't emulate their style. With your outside foot at the 6 o'clock position you are able to drive your weight down through the pedal, pushing the rear wheel into the ground. In this position, your rear wheel is planted solidly and is very unlikely to skid or slip out from underneath you.

You're now set up to take the corner perfectly. As you enter the corner, it tightens - move towards the apex staying relaxed and in position. Then, as you exit, you move to the outside of the bend, your body rightens towards vertical and you can start to pedal to regain speed. Now, look ahead and prepare for the next bend.

Unusual Situations

You now know how to take a corner, but what you do need to do is practice – a lot! Remember, you don't need a long mountain descent for practice. Riding a simple loop with lots of corners – perhaps on a local industrial estate – will give ample scope to practice. As you practice and gain exposure to a greater variety of corners, you'll discover some situations where the basic approaches to cornering don't quite give you everything you need to smoothly make the turn. The following are some scenarios that you may experience and how to deal with them.

"It's not the fastest rider who wins a downhill, it's the one who gets to the bottom in the shortest time."

François Gachet

Too Much Speed

Even the most experienced descenders occasionally find that they have too much speed as they enter a bend. If you are going too fast, simply hoping that you'll make it around the corner is not the best approach – do you really want to find out if your bike is going to slip out from underneath you? The instant you realise that you have too much speed, act. Brake to scrub speed. The bike will track straight as you do this, but you should lose enough speed to compensate. Remember that if you are leaning too much as you brake, the bike will lose traction and you'll both hit the deck!

Tightening Bends

Many bends follow a uniform arc which makes them easy to take. However, some tighten as they approach their apex. These types of bends, especially when blind, can easily catch a rider out who doesn't have local knowledge. Fortunately, you can compensate for this lack of knowledge by reading the road. As you enter a corner, look ahead at the white line along the centre of the road (or the outside edge of the road). If the amount of visible line is decreasing, the bend is tightening – position and brake accordingly. On the other hand, if the amount of visible line is increasing, the bend is slackening – you can relax and allow the bike to increase its speed.

Hairpins

You'll generally only find proper hairpin bends in mountainous areas. They show that the terrain is so steep that road builders had to make a succession of straights and turns to meander their way up the mountainside. Because they tend to steepen significantly at their mid-point and people ride them infrequently, they can be the most challenging of all bends. To take a hairpin, adopt the normal cornering approach whilst remembering to lose a lot of speed because you will gather speed as you corner due to the steepness of the road. You will still take a line of outside-inside-outside, but you will delay turning into the bend to create the best line. Figure 39 shows that you turn later into the bend and that the apex shifts from the mid-point of the bend to a point closer to the mid-point of the second part of the bend. Attaining the correct line takes experience and can be hard to judge. However, if you aim to be in the centre of the road (i.e. halfway between your inside and outside lines) at the mid-point of the bend, you will find that you are correctly positioned for the exit.

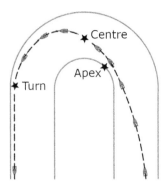

Figure 39 Cornering line for hairpin bends

Assessing the Environment

In a perfect world, every descent would be dry, have perfectly smooth tarmac and be free of traffic, potholes and other hazards. Alas, it's not a perfect world. Assessing road and weather conditions will allow you to descend smoothly without accident or incident.

The first thing to consider is the weather. If it's raining or the roads are wet, you need to slow your descent and brake earlier before entering corners. Wet roads can be slippery – your tyres will struggle to maintain traction – brake gently and don't lean too far in corners. Also, brakes are less effective so you'll need to allow even more time to compensate. Remember that ironwork and road markings become very slippery when wet, so you need to ensure that you don't come into contact with them. Finally, after periods of hot weather, especially in warm countries, patches of rubber form around corners and these dark patches can be extremely slippery.

If you're riding in winter conditions or in the high mountains, shaded areas may still contain areas of ice or snow. Both of these are exceptionally hard to traverse when cornering. If you do venture on any patches of snow or ice, ride extremely slowly and if you're in doubt, dismount and walk out the section – broken hips and collar bones are no fun. Another weather situation you are likely to encounter in the mountains is strong wind or gusts. A strong gust of wind can push a rider out into oncoming traffic or off the edge of a bend. When it's gusty, adjust your speed and make sure that you stay relaxed so that your body absorbs some of the gust rather than blowing you and your bike off course.

> **Good to Know:** When you climb, you become hot. Likewise, as you descend, you chill and can become cold. Ride with a gilet or race cape in your back pocket so that you can pop it on at the top of a climb to avoid the cold.

The second environmental consideration is road surface. Smooth tarmac allows you to descend with speed – rough surfaces jar your body and can throw your bike offline. If the road surface is rough, you'll need to reduce your speed –obviously! But, you can also improve the situation by following the lead of mountain bikers. These riders don't descend sat in the saddle, they're out of the saddle and using their feet. There's a reason for this: the suspension of mountain bikes allows their wheels to maintain contact with the ground – it's the rider's arms and legs that absorb the impact of the terrain. Of course, a road bike doesn't have suspension, so it is the rider that absorbs the irregularities of the road surface. If the surface is really rough, raise yourself slightly out of the saddle as you descend. With relaxed arms and legs, you'll comfortably and easily absorb everything that the road has to offer. Remember, though, that you have slightly raised your centre of gravity, so it is particularly important to ensure that you drive your weight through the pedals as you descend – remember the mountain bikers' maxim:

"Heavy Feet – Light Hands"

Anon

Thirdly and finally, you need to consider hazards on the road – you should never assume that a road is hazard free. The most obvious of hazards is other traffic. If the road's narrow, or a corner's blind, there's a chance that traffic may cross on to your side of the road. It makes sense to adjust your line and speed to ensure that you don't have an unexpected face-to-face meeting! Of course, there are many other hazards that you may encounter. The surface of mountain roads can often collect debris, such as rocks or branches. Likewise, some roads are plagued by potholes and many agricultural areas are prone to patches of mud. Always be prepared to modify your line and make sure you shout hazards out to following riders. In many areas, livestock or wild animals may wander on to the road - look out for signs warning motorists. Another sign to look for is 'Pedestrians'. Ramblers or pedestrians are often so engrossed in their thoughts or conversation that they fail to hear approaching cyclists. Expect the unexpected, they may be walking as a group in the carriageway or may suddenly step out in front of you.

Tackling Fear

On any popular descent you'll see people wracked with fear, hands grasping the brakes, their body in premature rigor mortis – they are besieged by blind panic. Where is the fun? What is the enjoyment? These people mark the opposite end of a spectrum that starts with those that have no fear and a reckless disregard for their own lives. Having a healthy pinch of caution can be prudent - being gripped by fear is debilitating. In fact, it is worse – fear can be dangerous. It's fear that makes people tense, which makes them grab at brakes and make poor choices of line. If you find that you're sitting at the wrong end of the reckless-fearful spectrum, don't worry. In this chapter you have discovered all of the techniques that will allow you to descend safely and without incident. You need to practice them and make them second nature. Trust the techniques, your bike and your own abilities. Dismiss dark thoughts as you descend, focus on the positive – the enjoyment. If there's an edge or a drop by the side of the road, don't worry – would you fall off the road if you were walking? Keep your eyes focused on the road ahead, not on what's over the edge of the road! Finally, if you feel that you are totally paralysed by fear, consider investing in some private coaching – you owe it to yourself to enjoy the entire ride, not just its end!

Good to Know: Regardless of your cornering ability, you can improve by riding with a more experienced companion. Ask them to descend slightly slower than normal and then follow their line. Copy the lines they take and the way that they position themselves on the bike. Following a controlled, faster rider will improve your technique, make you faster and give you more confidence.

Descending with Others

The "Riding with Others" chapter of this book explores riding with other cyclists. It contains important information that is essential to descending as well as other types of riding. That said, there are some safety considerations that are particular to descending:

- Avoid racing – it's tempting to harness the speed of the descent to start racing with your mates – especially if some of them left you clambering up the preceding climb. Racing pushes you to take chances and ride to the limit of your abilities. When you ride like this, if you encounter unexpected conditions or hazards, you have nowhere else to go. Just like a climb, take the descent at your own pace.

- Keep your distance – greater speeds require more distance to react and brake. Allow several bike lengths between you and the next rider. Too close and you won't be able to react.

- Don't tailgate – sometimes on descents, other vehicles can slow your progress – perhaps a cautious motorist or a tourist enjoying the scenery. Riders who follow these vehicles closely put themselves in a very dangerous position. Remember that cars, for example, have incredibly powerful brakes and can stop in a fraction of the time of a cyclist.

- Overtake with care – it's tempting to overtake a slow vehicle that impedes your descent. Generally, it's safer to sit back and accept your fate. If you do choose to overtake, ensure that you have sufficient visibility and space and avoid overtaking through a bend. Remember that the driver may not have seen you behind them. Give them plenty of space and be ready to react to sudden changes in speed.

Coping with Speed Wobble

Speed wobble is one of the most frightening things that you can experience when riding a bike. It's a strange phenomenon where your bike starts to oscillate, spasming underneath you. There is a lot of debate to what exactly causes this. True speed wobble is caused by the lateral oscillation of the frame's headtube. However, an equally unappealing sensation can be caused by other factors, such as:

- The frame's alignment.
- Inconsistencies in tyres or wheels.
- A rider's position on the bike.
- Loose or badly adjusted bearing – wheels or headset.

Whichever sensation you experience, it's a sensation you don't want. Fortunately, there are a number of techniques that may stop it before you and your bike part company:

1. Brake and slow down – often not that effective, unfortunately.
2. Pedal - speeding up may seem counterintuitive but pedalling often works.
3. Relax – tension will only make the situation worse.
4. Unweight the saddle.

Luckily, speed wobble is a rarity. If you ever experience it, the first thing you should do is take your bike for a service to check that all bearings are correctly adjusted and that there are no other problems with the bike. If this does not resolve the issue, try a different combination of wheels and tyres or even a slight modification to your bike position. If all else fails, you may have to accept that your bike's frame is simply not working for you – it could be time for a different bike!

Rounding Up

In this chapter, you discovered the basics of descending - being relaxed on the drops, foot position and line choice. You then explored other descending scenarios including rough roads, hairpin bends, reading the road and dealing with excess speed. Finally, you learnt about safety and how to deal with speed wobble.

Maintaining Your Bike

If you could see some of the bikes that end up in cycle workshops, you'd cry. Once beautiful machines that were the pride and joy of their owners have been abused, misused and denied any form of maintenance. Now they creak, squeak and grind their way towards a premature grave. There reaches a point where a bike simply becomes uneconomical to repair and when that's the result of neglect rather than age, that's a sad thing. You don't need to be a mechanic to keep your bike in good condition, but you do have to go a little beyond pumping up the tyres occasionally and drowning the chain in oil once a year. In this chapter, you'll discover the essential aspects of bike maintenance and how to test for problems.

"Don't buy upgrades. Ride up grades."

Eddy Merckx

Tools

Professional bike mechanics have a huge number of tools at their disposal which allow them to perform almost any repair on any bicycle. The majority of these tools are specific to a given task or model of component and even a professional may only use some of these tools once or twice a year. In common with other specialist equipment, the cost of some of these tools can be very high – a professional toolkit can cost thousands of pounds. Fortunately, for home maintenance, you only need a small number of tools and these are quite low-cost. In fact, most of the tools you can buy in any hardware store for just a few pounds. The following list provides you with an essential home maintenance toolkit:

- Allen keys – most bolts on modern road bikes require an Allen key. The essential sizes are 4, 5, and 6 mm, however buying a set ranging from 2 mm to 10 mm is a good investment. A basic Allen key set, as found in a hardware store, will suffice, but if you spend a little more, you can buy a p-handled set, which is easier to work with.

- Screwdrivers – a Philips #2 screwdriver will allow you to complete most jobs on the bike. However, owning a Philips #1 and flatheads #1 and #2 may also be useful.

- Tyre levers – a set of two or three plastic tyre levers are essential for removing tyres. Buy these from your local bike shop or online.

- Pump – a handpump will suffice, but a track pump makes life much easier when it comes to attaining the high pressures required by road bikes.

> **Good to Know:** There are several 'bicycle toolkits' on the market. These toolkits provide a selection of tools for the home mechanic. Unfortunately, it's almost guaranteed that some of the tools won't be applicable to your bike and, frequently, the quality of the remaining tools may be poor. Save money by buying just what you actually need.

In addition to the essential tools, there are two items that can make home repairs easier and more accurate:

1. Workstand – a workstand holds your bike up from the floor and allows you to work on your bike without kneeling on the floor or holding it with one hand as you try to complete an operation that requires both hands. Professional workstands cost several hundred pounds, but lightweight home versions are available from bike shops and online for less than a hundred pounds. A little luxury that will make life much easier – highly recommended.

2. Torque wrench – you should tighten the bolts and fixings on your bike to a specific amount of force (known as torque). A torque wrench is a tool that allows you to set a specific torque and as you tighten a bolt, it will produce an audible click when you reach the specified torque. If you have bought a carbon road bike, spending £50 or £60 on

131

an entry-level torque wrench is a wise investment and represents a fraction of the cost of replacing broken components or a frame. If you've bought an entry-level bike, although nice to have, a torque wrench may be a little too luxurious for now.

Technique

Road bike components are expensive and many of them are fragile. A heavy-handed approach to maintenance is likely to cause damage and unnecessary expense. So, before you begin, here's a small number of rules that may save you unnecessary expense and visits to the bike shop:

1. **Clean before you start** – a clean bike is more pleasant to work on, problems present themselves more clearly and tools work better on clean components. The Cleaning section of this chapter explains how to clean your bike.

2. **Keep organised** – lay out your tools before you begin so they're at hand when you need them. If you remove parts from your bike, lay them out in a logical order on a clean surface. If you're working on something new or complex, take a photo before you start and that way you'll have a record of how things fit together.

3. **Avoid force** – there are very few parts of a bike that require significant force to loosen or tighten and working with these parts is beyond the scope of this book. If you feel that you need excessive force, refer to rule #5.

4. **Keep hammers for hammering** – there are very few instances when a hammer and a bike should come in to contact and all of these instances relate to topics beyond the scope of this book.

5. **Remember: Lefty Loosey Righty Tighty** – almost all nuts and bolts that secure components comply with this maxim. There are a small number of exceptions and this chapter highlights these when they occur.

6. **Check everything** – always check your work. Methodically check each nut, bolt or quick release to ensure that you haven't missed one in your excitement to get back on the road.

Cleaning

There are some cyclists who, after each ride, strip their bikes and meticulously clean each component. If that's their thing, good for them. However, this level of cleaning is not necessary on a regular basis. That said, basic cleaning of your bike is a good idea. A clean bike looks good, operates smoothly and efficiently and during the process of cleaning provides you with an opportunity to spot problems and wear.

The golden rule of bike cleaning is never to use a jet wash. It may seem appealing to wash away all the dirt and grime with the minimum of effort but there's a hidden dark side. Jet washes create a pressurised jet of water and this water finds its way into the bearings of your bike. After a few months of regular jet washing, the grease packed around all the bearings in your bike's bottom bracket, headset and wheels' hubs will disappear. Before you know it, you'll be faced with an expensive repair bill or a bike that feels awful to ride.

The correct approach is to use a dedicated bike cleaning product such as MucOff that eliminates grime and dirt whilst not attacking bearings. If you don't have a cleaning product, or would rather save your money for coffee stops, you can simply use a bucket of warm water. Using a soft cloth or sponge, start at the top of the bike and work your way down, carefully cleaning as you go. At this point, avoid the chain because you'll quickly have an oily mess and a ruined sponge. Once clean, wash away any residual cleaning product and then take a soft rag and dry your bike so that water doesn't sit on bolts and cause rust.

To clean the chain and cassette you'll need to take a different approach. You can buy a chain cleaner (a dedicated device that cleans your chain with the minimum amount of mess) – most bike shops stock these. Alternatively, you can buy a chain cleaning product (often in aerosol format) and use this together with some old rags. Once the chain is clean, give the cassette a scrub with either a dedicated cassette cleaning tool (a specially shaped brush) or an old toothbrush. Ensure that all cleaning products are thoroughly removed so that they don't seep through to your rear wheel bearings.

Your bike should be clean now so all that's left is to lube and protect. Apply your chosen chain lube as described in the next section of this chapter. You can also apply a drop of oil to the springs and pivot points of your derailleurs. Then, optionally, give your bike a spray with a PTFE product to make everything shine and provide additional protection against the elements and dirt. Bike shops use GT85 for this purpose – do not use traditional WD40 or similar because this will strip grease. Importantly, remember to avoid spraying your chain and cassette (you'll degrade the lube that's on them) and the wheels' rims and brake pads (you'll lose braking performance).

Lubricating Chains

Now that you have cleaned your bike, it's time to check the chain. A series of rollers and rivets make up a chain and these need lubrication to move smoothly. A chain that lacks lubrication is not only inefficient, it will wear quickly and it can make a truly annoying squeaking noise as you pedal. On the other hand, a chain with too much lubrication will splash oil on to you and your bike, attract debris that wears the chain and find its way into the rear wheel bearings washing out grease and creating expensive premature wear within the wheel's hub. Luckily, it's easy to check whether you have the correct amount of lube. Glide your finger over the top of the chain and assess as follows:

- Clean finger: you need lube.
- Light oil marks: it's perfect.
- Covered in oil: too much lube.

To lubricate the chain, lift the rear wheel and hold the lube bottle adjacent to the chain (see Figure 40). Turn the pedals and allow the oil to slowly drizzle over each link. Once each link has a light coating, put the oil down and spin the pedals a few times – you're done. If you accidentally apply too much lube, gently hold a rag around the chain and slowly turn the pedals. The rag will absorb the excess oil and your chain should be perfectly lubricated.

Figure 40 Lubricating a chain

Good to Know: Always use cycle chain oil or lube. It has the correct viscosity for the chain, whereas greases and very fine lubes do not. Lubes start with a basic cycle oil and progress through to lubes for specific conditions: dry (for mostly dry conditions) and wet (for very wet conditions). Some premium lubes are wax-based. These allow particles of debris to stick to the wax and shed as they become too numerous. Do not apply wax to an oiled chain and vice versa.

Tyres

Tyres are the contact points between your bike and the road. They have a huge influence on your performance, comfort and safety. Before each ride, check the air pressure of both tyres. They lose a small amount of pressure over time and low pressures hinder performance and adversely affect your control of the bike when braking or cornering. The side wall of the tyre shows one of the following: a recommended pressure, a maximum pressure or a minimum pressure. This will be expressed either as PSI (pounds per square inch) or Bar (continental measurement of pressure). If you can't find this, you can use the guide in Table 4:

Rider Weight (lbs)	Front Tyre	Rear Tyre
110	85	90
140	95	105
180	105	110

Table 4 Suggested tyre pressures

Note: Based on a 700 x 23 c tyre
Note: Never exceed the maximum pressure stated on the tyre

Some people think that pumping up tyres to the maximum pressure will achieve the greatest speed. This is a myth because although the bike will roll faster as the tyre pressure increases, it will reach a point where the tyre and bike will bounce off the road surface and hinder performance.

Once you have made any adjustments to tyre pressure, examine both tyres for damage and excessive wear. Small marks and holes (maybe 1 mm in diameter) are normal. However, larger holes, cracked side walls or bulges are of concern because the structure of the tyre may be compromised. If you see any damage of this nature, replace the tyre or ask your local bike shop for their opinion. A damaged tyre may collapse or explode, and this is likely to cause an adverse connection between you and the road – do not ride on them!

It's easy to check a tyre for wear whilst you're checking for damage. Unlike a vehicle tyre, most road bike tyres have no tread, so you cannot gauge wear from tread depth. Instead, you examine the profile of the tyre. Figure 41 shows two tyre profiles, on the left you can see the rounded profile of a tyre with plenty of wear remaining and on the right, you'll notice that the centre of the tyre has become flattened indicating excessive wear. As a rule of thumb, once a tyre's profile feels flat, it needs replacing.

Rounded profile   Flattened profile

Figure 41 Tyre wear

Good to Know: Rear tyres wear at a much faster rate than front tyres because of the rider's weight distribution. Do not be tempted to switch front and rear tyres to increase their lifespan. A worn front tyre drastically affects a bike's handling and can seriously impact its ability to corner safely.

Figure 42 Flip the brake quick release to up

Figure 43 Release the wheel's quick release

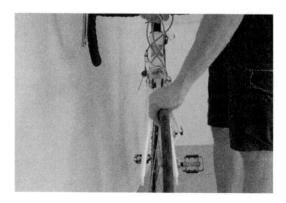

Figure 44 Remove the wheel

Wheel Removal

Removing the wheels of your bike is an essential skill that fills many people with dread. If you know how, wheel removal is simple but if you don't, it's easy to find yourself battling with your bike's chain and becoming covered in oil. In this section you'll learn the easiest methods for removing and refitting wheels so next time you need to pop your bike in the car or you suffer a puncture, you'll know exactly what to do.

Removing a Front Wheel

Front wheels are the easiest to remove. To remove the wheel:

1. **Flip the brake quick release to the up position** - Figure 42. This will ensure that the brake pads do not catch on the tyre as you remove the wheel. If you have disc brakes, you can skip this step.

2. **Release the wheel's quick release** - Figure 43. Flip the quick release lever and then whilst holding the nut on the opposing side of skewer, turn the lever anti-clockwise a few turns. You do not need to completely undo the quick release, this will result in the springs of the quick release pinging off on to the side of the road.

3. **Remove the wheel.** - Figure 44. Hold the wheel with one hand and, with the other, lift the front of the bike away from the wheel. If the wheel does not come free, loosen the quick release another turn or two.

Figure 45 Refit the wheel

Figure 46 Tighten the wheel's quick release

Figure 47 Flip the brake's quick release down

Refitting a Front Wheel

Refitting a front wheel is easy, but it's important that it is done correctly. A badly fitted front wheel may affect braking or steering. To refit the wheel:

1. **Refit the wheel** - Figure 45. Hold the wheel with one hand and lift the front of the bike with the other. Slowly lower the bike so that the fork dropouts engage with the front wheel. Note that if your wheel has a tyre with tread, ensure that the wheel is correctly orientated – the sidewall of the tyre will have an arrow that points to the forward direction of travel.

2. **Tighten the quick release** - Figure 46. Keeping the bike and the wheel upright, hold the quick release with one hand whilst turning the opposing nut with the other. To test if the quick release is tightened correctly, close the quick release lever. The adjustment is correct if you have to use a little pressure and the quick release lever leaves an imprint in the palm of your hand. You should never force the lever or use tools on any part of the quick release. If, on the other hand, the lever closes with little or no resistance, you need to release it and tighten it further.

3. **Flip the brake quick release lever to the down position** - Figure 47. If you watch the brake as you do this, you'll see that the brake pads move in closer to the rim. This ensures that you have the full power of the brake. If you do forget this step, your brake will still work but you will have to pull the lever further until the brake engages.

4. **Test.** Squeeze the brake lever and release. Lift the front of the bike and spin the front wheel. If the wheel spins freely, you're done. If the wheel rubs the brake or seems to move from side to side, pop the bike back on the ground and check that you have fitted the wheel correctly.

Figure 48 Move the chain on to the smallest cog

Figure 49 Grasp the rear derailleur

Figure 50 Hold the derailleur and remove the wheel

Removing a Rear Wheel

Rear wheels are less straightforward than front wheels to remove, but there's a little trick that you'll learn that'll make you look like a professional mechanic – here's how:

1. **Change gear** - Figure 48. Lift the rear of the bike and by hand, pedal as you drop down the gears. You want the chain to sit on the inner chain-ring at the front and on the smallest cog of the rear cassette. With the chain in this position, there is very little tension on the rear derailleur and you'll find wheel removal much easier.

2. **Flip the brake quick release to the up position.**

3. **Release the wheel's quick release.**

4. **Remove the wheel.** Hold the rear of the bike with one hand and with the other grasp the rear derailleur, as shown in Figure 49 and Figure 50, and gently pull it backwards towards you. Lift the bike and the wheel will cleanly detach without becoming tangled in the chain.

5. **Note to self.** Remember to never rest the rear of your bike directly on the ground without a wheel. The rear derailleur is fragile and resting it on the ground may result in damage. Instead, rest your bike on its side.

Good to Know: Professional mechanics can change a wheel within a few seconds. This is because they have repeated the process so many times it has become automatic. Give yourself a professional edge by practicing at home until you can remove and refit your wheels without thinking.

Figure 51 Hold derailleur clear of the cassette

Figure 52 Engage chain and cassette

Refitting a Rear Wheel

In common with rear wheel removal, refitting is trickier than the front. However, because you changed down the gears when you removed the wheel, you'll find the process of refitting straightforward.

1. **Refit the wheel.** With the rear wheel steadied between your legs, hold the rear of the bike with one hand. With your other hand, grasp the rear derailleur, as shown in Figure 51 and Figure 52, and gently pull it backwards towards you. Lift the bike over the rear wheel and allow the chain to engage with the teeth of the smallest cog. Lower the bike and gently release the derailleur so that the chain wraps neatly around the smallest cog.

2. **Tighten the quick release.**

3. **Flip the brake quick release lever to the down position.**

4. **Test.** Lift the rear of your bike and turn the pedals by hand to ensure that chain is properly engaged with the teeth of the cassette and chain-ring. If the wheel turns and does not touch the brake pads, change the rear gears so that the chain sits somewhere around the middle of the cassette. Doing this ensures that you are in an appropriate gear to start riding when you jump back on your bike.

Good to Know: Never ride your bike with flat tyres. You may be tempted to limp your bike along the road before stopping and addressing a puncture but riding on flat tyres will damage your wheels' rims and can result in a tyre or inner tube becoming tangled in your bike's moving parts.

Punctures

Some people seem to be plagued by punctures and others ride for years without one. If you ride in an area where hedge trimming takes place, you will be prone to more punctures because trimmings often contain thorns that have a magic ability to pierce tyres. Equally, if you ride in an urban setting and ride too close to the edge of the road, you'll roll through debris that may contain fragments of metal or glass that can easily puncture a tyre. Regardless of where you ride, you will drastically reduce the chances of puncturing by investing in quality tyres and keeping them correctly inflated.

If you do puncture when out on a ride, or you discover your bike has lost a lot of tyre pressure since your last ride, you need to decide what type of puncture you've suffered. Generally speaking, there are three types of puncture:

1. A slow – your tyre loses air slowly, perhaps over a period of hours or days. Sometimes this is a result of tiny holes in the inner tube and other times it's because of a leaky inner tube valve. Either way you'll need to replace the inner tube. It's worth remembering that if you're out on a ride, you may be able to pump up your tyre once or twice and make it back home.

2. A regular puncture – your tyre loses air quickly perhaps over a period of seconds or minutes. This type of puncture is generally the result of a foreign object piercing your bike's tyre and inner tube. You'll need to stop and repair or replace the inner tube.

3. A blowout – your tyre loses air rapidly, often accompanied by a bang and a sudden loss of bike control. This is often the result of an impact on the tyre, which traps the inner tube between the tyre and your wheel's rim – hence this is often known as a pinch flat. The most common causes of this are riding into a pothole or riding with under inflated

tyres. You'll need to stop quickly to avoid damaging your wheel's rim.

> **Good to Know:** You should always replace an inner tube rather than repair one that's damaged. The high pressures required by road bikes mean that a repaired inner tube is not as safe as a new inner tube. However, if you're out on a ride and suffer multiple punctures, you can use a patched inner tube to get you home. All good bike shops sell glueless puncture repair patches that simply require you to identify the hole, roughen the affected area with sandpaper and apply a patch – no glue, no mess, no waiting.

When you do puncture, pull to the side of the road and let the people you're riding with know that you've got a flat. Before you start to address the problem, ensure that you are in a safe place to work on your bike. If not, push your bike to the nearest place of safety. Once you're ready, remove the wheel, as explained earlier in this chapter, and follow these steps to replace your inner tube:

1. **Clear remaining air** - Figure 53. Loosen the valve nut and depress it. This will clear the inner tube of any remaining air.

2. **Remove tyre from one side of the rim.** Insert the end of a tyre lever between the edge of the rim and the tyre. Pull the lever back towards the centre of the wheel. In many cases you'll now be able to slide the lever around the rim, freeing the bead of the tyre. If this is not possible, you'll need to insert a second tyre lever a couple of inches from the first. You should now be able to slide this second lever around the rim and free the tyre's bead. Once one bead of the tyre is free, stop. There's no need to remove the tyre.

$\rightarrow$

Figure 53 Clear remaining air

Figure 54 Remove inner tube

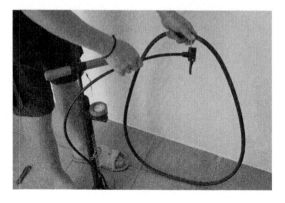

Figure 55 Pre-inflate inner tube

Figure 56 Fit inner tube

Figure 57 Refit tyre

Figure 58 Check tyre is seated

3. **Remove inner tube** - Figure 54. Starting opposite the valve grab the inner tube and pull it out from the wheel. Although you're going to replace this inner tube, roll it up and keep it either as an emergency spare or to dispose of when you get back home.

4. **Check tyre.** Carefully run your fingers around the inside of the tyre, feeling for foreign bodies. Remember to do this slowly because anything sharp enough to pierce a tyre may cut your fingers.

5. **Remove debris.** Remove any foreign objects you find. Remember that more than one item may have pierced your tyre, so check carefully. Equally, sometimes the object that pierced the tyre does not remain in the tyre so there will be nothing to find.

6. **Pre-inflate inner tube** - Figure 55. Loosen the valve nut of a new inner tube and attach your pump. Inflate the inner tube just enough to give it its shape. This helps ensure that you don't accidently pinch the inner tube when you refit the tyre to the wheel's rim.

7. **Fit inner tube** - Figure 56. Insert the valve of the inner tube through the hole in the wheel's rim and then slowly work the inner tube into the space between the tyre and rim. Ensure that the inner tube is neatly positioned with no sections sticking out beyond the rim and the tyre. Finally, push the valve of the inner tube up and down to ensure that none of the inner tube is caught beneath or around it.

8. **Refit tyre bead** - Figure 57. Starting by the valve, use your thumbs to ease the tyre bead back on to the rim. Work from side to side so that the final gap is opposite the valve. You may find that the final section of bead is too hard for you to push with your thumbs. If this is the case, you can use a plastic tyre lever inserted backward between the rim and tyre and use a pushing motion to pop the tyre back on to the rim.

$\rightarrow$

9. **Check** - Figure 58. Turn the wheel in your hands visually checking that the tyre is correctly fitted to the rim.

10. **Re-inflate.** Start inflating the tyre but stop when you reach approximately 20 psi or 1 bar. Visually check the tyre again to ensure that it is sat correctly on the rim and that there's no inner tube sticking out. If everything is OK, continue pumping to your normal pressure. You can now refit your wheel as described earlier in this chapter.

Basic Adjustments

There are a few basic adjustments that every cyclist should be able to complete competently, and, if you read the "Getting the Right Fit" chapter, you will need to perform some of these adjustments, such as changing saddle height. The following sections tell you how and, importantly, help you avoid costly mistakes.

Saddle

A saddle secures to a seatpost through a clamping mechanism which also allows the rider to adjust the tilt of the saddle. Almost all road bikes use a system that relies on Allen key bolts to adjust and secure the saddle. There are two commonly used systems; the first has Allen key bolts located underneath the saddle (bottom clamp) and the second has them located on the side of the saddle (side clamp). In both cases do not completely undo the retaining bolts because it can be fiddly, and incredibly frustrating, to put the clamping mechanism back together again. To adjust a bottom clamp:

1. **Look** underneath the saddle and you will see two Allen key bolts that secure the clamp around the saddle rails.

$\rightarrow$

2. **Loosen both bolts** by a couple of turns so that you can tilt the saddle with your hand.

3. To move the nose of the saddle down, loosen the bolt at the nose end a further couple of turns.

4. To move the nose of the saddle up, loosen the bolt at the rear of the saddle a further couple of turns.

5. **Tighten both bolts** incrementally. Notice that as each bolt tightens, it tends to tilt the saddle one way or the other. Tightening or loosening each bolt, as described in the previous step, will allow you to get your desired tilt.

6. **Complete tightening** to ensure that the saddle does not move when you ride. Saddle clamps generally need to be quite tight. If you have a torque wrench, the torque is normally in the range of 10-12 Nm (it may be printed on the saddle clamp). If you don't have a torque wrench, you'll need to tighten the bolts using some muscle but not to the point where you risk damaging the heads of the bolts.

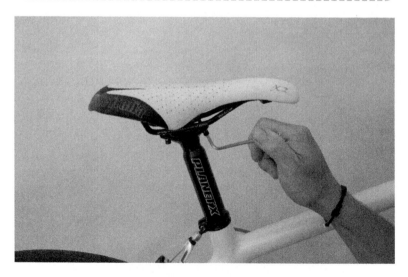

Figure 59 Bottom clamp saddle fitment

To adjust a side clamp mechanism:

1. **Look** at either side of the saddle and you will see either one or two Allen key bolts that secure the clamp around the saddle.
2. **Loosen the bolt(s)** by a couple of turns so that you can tilt the saddle with your hand. You may find that the saddle does not move freely. This is common and easily fixed by holding both the nose and rear of saddle and giving it a firm rock.
3. **Tilt the saddle** to your preferred angle and tighten the clamp bolt(s).
4. **Complete tightening** to ensure that the saddle does not move when you ride. Saddle clamps generally need to be quite tight. If you have a torque wrench, the torque is normally in the range of 10-12 Nm (it may be printed on the saddle clamp). If you don't have a torque wrench, you'll need to tighten the bolts using some muscle but not to the point where you risk damaging the heads of the bolts.

Seatpost

Adjusting your seatpost allows you to adjust both saddle rotation, i.e. which direction it's pointing and saddle height. Most seatposts are secured to a bike's frame by a clamp, which is a small collar that stops the seatpost sliding down when you sit on your bike. This clamp will have either one or two bolts that secure it. To adjust:

1. **Loosen the clamp bolt(s)** enough to be able to rotate the seatpost by twisting the saddle (normally a couple of turns). If the clamp is loose and your seatpost won't move, you may have a seized seatpost – the seatpost

→

has fused to the interior of the frame – and you'll need to get a mechanic to release it.

2. **Twist/lift/push the saddle** to move the seatpost in the position or direction you want.

3. **Tighten the seatpost clamp**. If your clamp has two bolts, tighten each a little in turn so that they are tightened evenly. Whether you have one bolt or two, it's important that you don't overtighten the clamp because you risk damaging your bike's frame. If you have a torque wrench, the torque is normally in the range of 4-6 Nm (it should be printed on the seatpost clamp). If you don't have a torque wrench, you'll know that you've got the correct tightness when you can no longer twist the saddle from side to side by hand.

Figure 60 Don't overtighten seatpost clamp bolt

Stem

The stem of your bike connects your handlebar to the steering column of the fork. If your stem becomes misaligned, perhaps as the result of a crash, you'll need to be able to realign it. This is an important task because if you don't do it correctly, you could lose control of steering. To adjust the stem's rotation:

1. **Loosen stem bolts** – on either side of the stem there is a bolt that clamps the stem to the steering column. Loosen each bolt a turn at a time so as to keep even pressure between them. You'll need to loosen them two or three complete turns. Do not touch the bolt that sits above the stem – this is to adjust the headset bearings.

2. **Rotate the stem** – stand over your bike and move its handlebar until the stem aligns perfectly with the front wheel. →

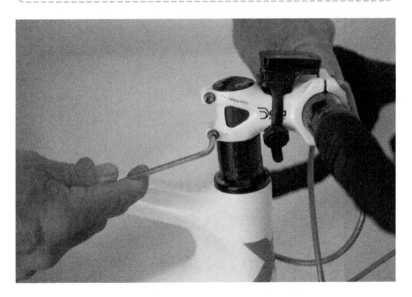

Figure 61 Location of stem bolt(s)

3. **Tighten stem bolts** – take turns to tighten each bolt ensuring that you don't accidently move the stem or front wheel as you do this. Stem bolts should not be →

too tight because you risk damaging the top of your fork's steering column. If you have a torque wrench, the torque is normally in the range of 4-7 Nm (it should be printed on the stem). If you don't have a torque wrench, tighten the bolts so that you use a little muscular force but are not forcing the tool. You can check that the bolts are adequately tight by positioning the front wheel between your legs whilst facing the handlebar and then firmly trying to twist the handlebar from side to side. If the handlebar moves the stem out of line with the front wheel, the bolts are not tight enough.

Pedals

If you're travelling with your bike, or just bought some new pedals, you'll need to be able to remove and fit your bike's pedals. A lot of people run into trouble when trying to remove pedals and this is because they don't realise that the pedals have opposing threads, i.e. one tightens by turning to the right and the other to the left. To avoid any problems, remove them with this procedure:

1. **Select the correct tools** – to remove your pedals you will either require a 15 mm spanner or an Allen key (typically 6 or 8 mm) depending on your pedals' fixings.

2. **Loosen both pedals a couple of turns** – stand behind your bike and turn the tool towards you (it's the same for both sides). The initial turn may require some effort if your pedals haven't been removed for some time or were over tightened when last fitted. Take care on the drive side (right hand-side) that you don't catch your arm on the teeth of the chainring – ouch!

$\rightarrow$

3. **Remove pedals** – continue to undo the pedals until they come away from the bike. It's a good idea to hold the pedals as you reach the end of loosening them so that they don't fall on to the floor. Sometimes there's a thin washer than sits between the pedal and the crankarm – look out for these because they are easily missed.

Figure 62 Remember that the left hand pedal has a reverse thread

It's simple to fit pedals, just:

1. **Grease the threads of the pedal axle** – lightly coating the threads of the pedal axles helps prevent pedals seizing, ensures that you can tighten them adequately and helps eradicate squeaks when the pedals are under load. Your local bike shop will have

→

suitable grease but in reality, almost any grease will suffice.

2. **Mount the pedals** – by hand, start to thread the pedals back on the crankarms. You must turn both the pedals toward the front of the bike – remember that they are threaded in opposite directions and as such each pedal is marked 'L' (left) or 'R' (right). If the pedal does not thread easily, remove it and try again – you may have cross threaded the pedal (the threads are not in line) and forcing it will cause significant damage.

3. **Tighten pedals** – pedals need to be tight. You'll need to put some effort into the final turn but not so much as you are straining under the effort or that it feels that the tool may damage a fixing.

Brakes

Brakes offer the great benefit of slowing and stopping your bike without you having to jump off to stop – an excellent invention. They operate best when cables and pads are in good condition and properly adjusted. Traditionally, road bike brakes are of the calliper variety (Figure 63) where the rider squeezes the brake lever which in turn pulls a cable that pulls the brake callipers allowing the brake pads to contact the wheel's rim. In recent years, disc brakes have become popular on some road bikes, especially those with endurance geometry. There are two main types of disc brake both of which rely on small pads that are housed in the brake calliper body and contact a brake disc to slow the bike:

1. Cable operated – a cable pulls one or both callipers allowing the brake pads to contact the disc.

2. Hydraulic systems – when the rider squeezes the brake lever, a fluid (DOT fluid or mineral oil) is pushed through a pipe that pushes pistons housed in the brake calliper, allowing the brake pads to contact the disc.

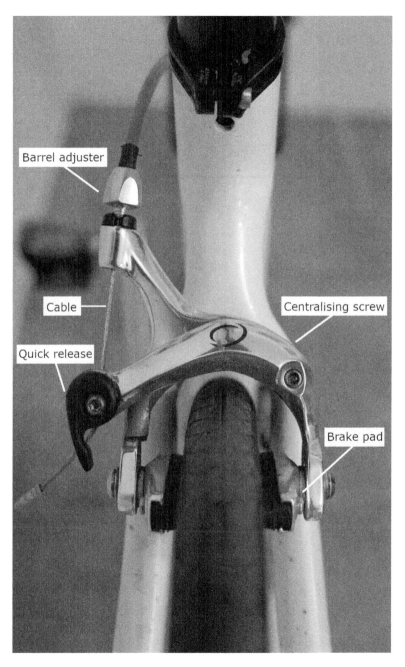

Figure 63 Calliper brake showing location of barrel adjuster, quick release and centralising screw

If your brake has a cable, inspect its visible parts from time to time. If it is corroded or has any damage at all, it needs replacing. Because the cable is so vital, it's a good idea to have your brake cables replaced on an annual basis as part of a service. Alternatively, if your brake is hydraulic, it should feel solid when you squeeze the brake lever. If it feels spongy or you have to squeeze the lever a few times to obtain a firm brake, there's air in the system. Air compresses and causes poor performance and potentially a loss of braking. You'll need to pop to your local bike shop to have the brakes bled (purges them of air).

All brake pads wear with time and must be replaced. It's easy to gauge wear on traditional brake blocks because you can see them. They may have a wear line to signal when to replace them or alternatively, if their surface has become smooth, it's time to replace them. Disc brake pads are harder to judge. You may be able to see the pads. If they have worn to a depth of one millimetre, replace them. Equally, if you hear any metallic noise when you brake, they need replacing.

> **Good to Know:** Never get oil, grease or lubricating spray near disc brake pads, calliper and disc. These will all contaminate the brake pads which creates a loud squealing noise each time you brake and can result in a loss of braking power.

To get the best performance from your brakes and have them feel how you like them (not too hard or soft), it's necessary to adjust them from time to time. If your bike has a hydraulic system, there's very little to adjust as the brake stays centred as the brake pads wear. If you do feel that something is not right with them, consult a bike mechanic – poorly executed repairs and adjustments can lead to brake failure! For those with mechanical disc brakes, it is a good idea to ask the retailer how the brake adjusts because there are several commonly used systems. Finally, for those with normal mechanical brakes, there are two main adjustments:

1. Calliper centralisation
2. Cable tension

Centralised brake pads will both make contact with the wheel's rim at the same time. If they don't, they'll pull the wheel to one side when you brake. Most brakes will have an adjusting screw or small bolt that allows the user to centralise the brake. Figure 63 shows an example of this adjuster. As you turn the adjuster, one or both brake callipers will move away or toward the rim. Make your adjustment, then squeeze the brake to test that it returns to its central position.

As pads wear, the calliper arms must travel further to allow the pads to meet the wheel's rim. This, in turn, means that you must pull the brake lever further in towards the handlebar. To adjust this amount of travel, the brake has a simple barrel adjuster (Figure 63). As you turn this anti-clockwise, the brake pads move toward the rim – firms up the brake. Conversely, clockwise turns move the pads away from the rim. Adjust and test your brakes until you are happy with their feel. If the barrel adjuster will not turn by hand, do not use a tool such as pliers to turn it. The thread of the adjuster is delicate and prone to snap with excessive force.

Although these are the basic adjustments of a brake, you may have noticed that your brakes have a small lever that you can flick up or down (Figure 63). Many people, including experienced cyclists, use this lever incorrectly as a way to adjust their brake. Its actual purpose is to move the calliper arms away from the wheel so that you can remove a wheel without the tyre snagging on the brake pads. Whenever you use this quick release, ensure that you flip it back when you reinstall the wheel otherwise your brakes will feel very soft.

Gears

The smooth efficient operation of a bike's gears makes riding a pleasure, whereas, badly adjusted or worn gears make an unpleasant and frustrating experience. For many people, gears are shrouded in mystery – something that they feel are beyond their knowledge. Although initial setup and then further adjustment of gears requires specific knowledge, they are not that complicated.

Most road bikes have two derailleurs (see Figure 64) – one at the front that shifts the chain between the chain-rings, and a second at the rear that shifts the chain between the cogs of the cassette. The shifters located on the handlebar pull or release a cable, which in turn interacts with the front or rear derailleur to effect a gear change. These derailleurs are, in effect, simply springs that the cable either elongates or releases. Correct adjustment of the derailleurs ensures that the cables have sufficient tension to allow the derailleurs to move the chain so that it sits in line with the chainrings and cassette.

Figure 64 Front and rear derailleurs

If you have a look at either of your bike's derailleurs, you'll notice that there are a pair of screws (or small bolts) which may be labelled 'H' and 'L'. These screws adjust how far the derailleur can move in either direction – these are limit screws. If your bike's gears were setup correctly initially, there is no need for you to ever touch them. Incorrect adjustment of the limit screws can result in a derailed chain, which can jam between the frame and chainrings or jam behind the cassette into the rear wheel's spokes causing significant damage. Leave the limit screws alone.

You may also notice that the rear derailleur has a third screw located separately to the limit screws. This is the 'B' screw and its role is to change the distance between the rear derailleur and the cassette. Mechanics use this to adjust for cassettes with different ranges. Just like the limit screws, this is an adjuster that you should never need to touch.

Figure 65 Adjusting rear derailleur cable tension

So that's plenty of things that you should not touch, but what can you actually adjust? Well, that's quite simple: each derailleur has a barrel adjuster that allows you to adjust cable tension. The rear derailleur's barrel adjuster is located where the cable enters the derailleur as shown in Figure 65. When you turn the adjuster anti-clockwise, you tighten the cable, and likewise when you turn it clockwise, you release cable tension. The front derailleur does not have a built-in adjuster. Instead, you will find that there is a barrel adjuster situated somewhere along the cable that runs from the gear shifter to the derailleur. This adjuster operates in the same way as that of the rear.

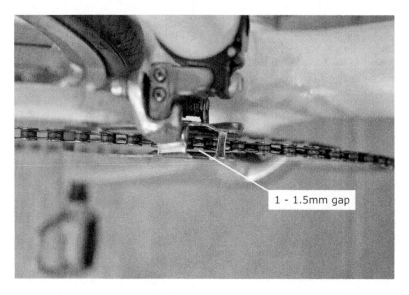

Figure 66 Front derailleur adjustment: Gap between chain and derailleur cage

To adjust the front derailleur, put your bike in a workstand or get an assistant to hold the saddle so as to lift the wheel from the ground. Turn the pedals by hand, changing the rear gears until the chain rests on the smallest cog. Shift the front derailleur so the chain sits on the big chain-ring (outer). Whilst pedalling, look between the outside plate of the derailleur and the chain. There should be a small gap of between 1 and 1.5 mm. If the chain is touching or catching the derailleur, turn the barrel adjuster anti-clockwise until it no longer touches. Now, change on to the small (inner) chain-ring and to the largest cog on the rear cassette. Whilst pedalling, view the gap between the chain and the inner face of the back plate of the derailleur. There should be a small gap of 1 to 1.5 mm between them. If the chain is touching or catching, the cable is too tight. Release a little tension by turning the barrel adjuster clockwise. Repeat this process until you are happy with the results. If you can't find a tension that works for both the small and big chain-ring, the derailleur may not have originally been setup correctly or it could be misaligned or misshapen. Pop to your local bike shop for an assessment.

To adjust the rear derailleur, change gear so that the chain sits on the small chain-ring. Now, shift the rear gears to the largest cog. If the derailleur cannot shift the chain to the largest cog, increase cable tension by turning the barrel adjuster anti-clockwise. With the chain on the largest cog, change gear to drop the chain down one cog. If the chain is hesitant or does not drop down, reduce cable tension by turning the barrel adjuster clockwise. If, on the other hand, the chain drops more than one cog, increase cable tension. Whilst making adjustments, you should only be making small adjustments to the barrel adjuster – say, one eighth or a quarter turn each time. Once the chain moves correctly between the two largest cogs, change gear moving up and down the entire rear gear range. Make very small adjustments until you obtain perfect indexing. If you can't find the correct adjustment there are several possible reasons, including a bent derailleur, bent gear hanger (see Figure 68), incorrectly adjusted limit or 'B' screws or damaged or worn gear cable. In these instances, you should pop down to your local bike shop for an assessment.

> **Good to Know:** Gear cables can attract grit and dirt and can degrade or rust over time. An affected cable will not move smoothly and result in poor shifting. Worse still, a damaged cable can snap, possibly resulting in an expensive repair such as the replacement of a gear shifter. Change your gear cables annually to avoid these problems.

Good to Know: A gear or mech hanger is a small piece of metal that connects a bike's rear derailleur to the bike's frame. The idea is that in the event of an impact, the hanger will bend or snap rather than the bike's frame. Because hangers are made of a soft material, they do occasionally get damaged inadvertently, for example by other bikes leaning against them. If a hanger is bent, the bike's rear gears will not operate correctly. To check if a hanger is bent, simply view your bike from behind. You should see that the rear derailleur hangs vertically below the cassette (see Figure 67.). If the cage of the derailleur is not vertical, you probably have a bent hanger. A mechanic will either realign the hanger or replace it whilst also ensuring that your gears are correctly adjusted.

Figure 67 Correctly aligned gear hanger

Bearings

Bearings are sets of metal or ceramic balls that are packed with grease. Their purpose is to allow parts of your bike to move freely and easily. The main bearings are present in the:

- Headset
- Bottom Bracket
- Wheels
- Pedals

Over time, moisture, grit and dirt access the bearings. Slowly this breaks down the grease and damages the shape of the bearings themselves. Some types of bearings can be repacked with grease periodically and others simply need to be replaced. Your bike shop will advise you based on your bike's particular components. Changing bearings can be fiddly and sometimes requires specialist tooling, but for you, it is helpful to be able to identify when a bearing is worn so that you can get it professionally replaced.

Starting with the headset, these bearings allow the front of the bike to pivot and in turn, allow you to steer. If the headset bearings wear excessively or seize, your steering may be adversely affected. Equally, if the adjustment of these bearings is incorrect, it may affect your steering and will cause premature wear or failure of components. To test headset bearings, many people pull the bike's front brake and try and rock the bike back and forth to check if there is play evident. This is not a good approach because any other play, for example within the brake or front wheel hub, will lead to a misdiagnosis. Luckily, checking headset bearings is simple:

1. With the bike on the ground, use one hand to hold the handlebar. With your other hand try to twist the spacers (Figure 68) that sit below or above the stem. If these turn, the headset is loose and needs adjusting.

167

2. Now, lift the bike by the handlebar so the front wheel is clear of the ground. Turn the handlebar from side to side. Does it turn smoothly? Good, there's no problem. Do you feel some resistance or a gritty sensation? If so, either the bearing adjustment is too tight or the bearings are worn.

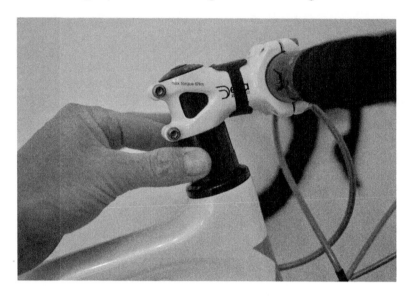

Figure 68 Checking headset adjustment

The bottom bracket bearings allow the cranks to turn and propel you forward. If they are worn, pedalling is less efficient and if badly worn, your bike and knees can be damaged. Testing for problems is simple:

1. Place your bike in a workstand or get an assistant to lift the bike by the saddle so that the rear wheel is clear of the ground. Using your fingers, lift the chain off the front chain-ring – change down to the inner chain-ring before doing this to reduce resistance. Gently spin the cranks by hand. If they turn smoothly – good, no problem. If there is resistance or a gritty feel, either the bearings are worn or are incorrectly adjusted.

2. Return the bike to the ground. With one hand, hold the frame to steady the bike. With the other, grasp either crank and try to move it back and forth in a direction perpendicular to the bike – see Figure 69 for clarification. There should be no movement. If there is any movement or knocking, there is a problem.

Figure 69 Testing bottom bracket bearings

Within each hub of the bike's wheels there are sets of bearings and these allow the wheels to rotate. If they are worn, the wheel will not turn smoothly and it will oscillate from side to side as you ride. This can be dangerous and it also increases the chances of spokes breaking. Additionally, badly worn bearings will ruin some brands of hub such as Shimano, and you'll have an expensive repair or replacement bill. To check bearings:

1. Place the bike in a workstand or have an assistant lift the bike. Spin each wheel in turn. The wheel should spin freely with no noise. If you hear a rumbling sound (more common in the rear wheel), your bearings either require cleaning and greasing or replacing.

2. Return the bike to the ground and hold the frame with one hand. With the other hand, grab the wheel and try to move it from side to side perpendicular to the direction the wheel rotates. There should be no movement. If there is movement or a knocking sound, your bearings either need adjustment or replacing.

Pedals contain several tiny bearings which allow the pedal to rotate or spin round. If these bearings are worn, the pedal may not turn properly and pedalling will be troublesome. In extreme cases, the body of the pedal can shear from the pedal axle, leaving the pedal and your foot disconnected from the bike. To test bearings:

1. Spin each pedal by hand and check that it moves freely with no noise. If they don't, and you have high-quality pedals, a mechanic may be able to adjust or replace the bearings. On the other hand, if you have cheaper pedals, you will need to replace them. Note that new pedals may not spin freely because of the amount of grease packed around the bearings – this is normal and not a problem.

2. Now, grab each pedal in turn and try to move it perpendicular to the bike as shown in Figure 70. It should not move and there should be no knocking. If it does, a mechanic may be able to adjust your pedals or you may have to replace them.

Chain Wear

Over time, the individual elements that make up a chain loosen and this has the effect of lengthening the chain. A worn chain results in poor performance, wears other components prematurely and is more likely to jump and fall off as you change gear. You can buy specific tools that indicate when a chain needs replacing but there is a simple method that provides a good indication. Take your bike and change gear so that the chain sits on the big chainring (the outer one) – it's not

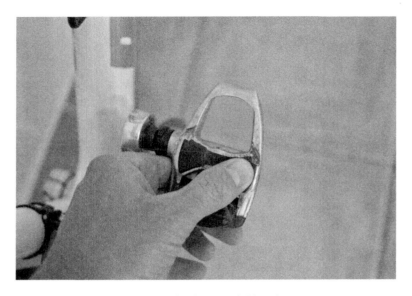

Figure 70 Checking pedal bearings

Figure 71 Checking chain wear

important where it sits on the rear cassette. Take the chain between your forefinger and thumb and gently try to pull it away from the chain-ring (see Figure 71). The chain will move away from the chain-ring, this is normal. If the chain moves, but still obscures the teeth of the chainring, it's fine. On the other hand, if you can see all or the majority of any chain-ring teeth, you'll need to replace the chain.

As the chain wears, so too does the cassette. This is because the spaces between each of the teeth on the cassette widen to match the elongated chain. This means that when you replace a chain, you should replace the cassette at the same time. If you don't, although it will work, you are likely to find that the chain will jump when you ride in certain gears, i.e. the ones that you use most often. The chain-rings also wear but because they are made of harder materials, they wear at a much slower rate. Normally, you will not need to replace these at the same time.

Services

If you own a car or a motorbike, you're used to the idea of having it serviced on a regular basis to keep it running smoothly and to avoid major mechanical problems. A bike is no different. And, just like a car, how often you have your bike serviced depends on mileage and time. For weekend riders, an annual service will suffice. For those that clock up higher mileage, services may be required two, three or four times per year.

The services that shops offer vary in what they include and, naturally, their price. If you feel that your bike needs some simple adjustment to brakes and gears, you can request a tune up where the mechanic will adjust your brakes and gears and, generally, identify any major issues with your bike. On the other hand, if it's been some time since your bike had a service, you should request a full service. In this instance, the mechanic will check and adjust all the components of your bike. Any components that are worn, will be identified and replaced and you'll be given advice on any components that are wearing, but not completely worn out. Some mechanics will routinely replace gear and brake cables, but others will only replace them if they are showing problems. Because cables are cheap and crucial to the safe and effective operation of your bike, each year you should request that they are changed.

There are also a few things that you can do to ensure that you get the best service and also help the shop's mechanic. The first is to remember that you need to book your bike in for a service – you need to wonder why a shop is so quiet if they can service your bike on the spot. It's worth remembering that lead times grow during the warmer months so don't be surprised if you have to book a few weeks in advance during the summer. The second is that if you know there are any issues, let the mechanic know beforehand. This allows the mechanic to ensure that any components required are in stock at the time. Thirdly, if you're worried about price, explicitly tell the shop to phone you if the service price is going to exceed a certain amount – this way you'll avoid any nasty surprises. Finally, when the shop tells you that your bike is ready for collection, collect it promptly. All shops struggle for storage space and a bike left for a long time is more likely to encounter accidental damage and also, it won't make you popular with the shop staff.

Rounding Up

In this chapter, you've explored the tools and techniques of the home mechanic. You've learnt how to keep your bike in optimum riding condition by cleaning, lubricating, and making adjustments to gears, brakes, saddle, seatpost and stem. You've also discovered how to correctly identify and deal with punctures of various kinds. You then moved on to identify common problems before they escalate and cause you or your bike serious damage. Finally, you took some tips on how to get the best out of a bike service.

Riding with Others

When you start riding, you may well ride alone but there will soon come a time that you'll want to ride with others. Riding in a group is more than a bunch of people riding together – it means complying to an unwritten code that is known to experienced riders. Initially, group riding can seem a little daunting and you can feel out of your depth – you're the new kid on the block. Don't worry. In this chapter you'll discover how to ride with others, what to say and some advanced group riding techniques.

*"A bicycle ride is
a flight from sadness."*

James E Starrs (Author)

Why Ride in a Group?

Some people spend their entire cycling life riding solo. This may work for them but for most people, group riding provides a more satisfying and fulfilling experience. Riding with a group of friends (or soon to become friends) provides a social element to what would otherwise be a solitary pursuit. The miles soon disappear when you can chat and take part in friendly banter as you roll. This social element is not only enjoyable but it also helps keep motivation high – it's much easier to drag yourself out of bed on a cold winter's morning to ride with a group than it is to head off on your own. Also, as you talk to people, you'll learn about techniques, upcoming events, new equipment and a whole plethora of new information.

Another very important benefit of group riding is that it easier than riding solo. An interesting phenomenon of cycling is that it requires less effort to ride behind someone than it does on your own. This is because the rider in front of you blocks some of the wind or air resistance meaning that you expend less energy to move at the same speed. This is known as drafting and if you watch cycle racing, you'll notice that sometimes the people at the front of the group (or peloton as it's called in cycling parlance) are pedalling hard whilst people further back in the peloton are simply coasting – they are in effect being sucked along by the riders up front.

Figure 72 Group riding

The Basics of Group Riding

The first time you ride in a group it can seem a little overwhelming – almost like you're in the middle of the peloton during the Tour de France. There are riders in front of you, to your side and behind. Everyone seems close and it feels like you're moving at quite a pace. If it's your first time in a larger group, you may be happier riding towards the rear of the group until you become more confident. That said, it won't be long until your mind settles and you feel more at home, and comfortable, in the middle of group.

Road Position

As you ride, you need to be aware of the people around you and the road ahead. This requires more concentration than riding solo. You hope that everyone is experienced and knows how to ride as a single entity but you cannot rely on this. Until you know particular riders well, do not assume that they know how to ride in a group. For example, an inexperienced rider may brake if they feel they are too close to the rider in front. If you're following their rear wheel too closely, you could easily crash into the back of them. Equally, you may panic and brake in reaction – the rider behind you may not be able to react so quickly.

Often groups ride two abreast (this is legal in most countries, regardless of some motorists' points of view) and this provides a nice setup for social exchanges. If you're a little nervous to start with, position yourself on the outside edge (closest to the centre of the road) because this gives you space to react if something happens. If you find yourself in a group that is riding more than two abreast, assuming that it is not a closed road, either move forward or backwards and away from these riders. This style of riding is generally not legal and is a lot more dangerous than riding two abreast.

If you are not at the front of the group, you will have another rider in front of you. The closer your front wheel is to their rear wheel, the less air resistance and the easier your ride. You need to assess how experienced that rider is and how likely they are to make some sudden unexpected move such as braking or swerving to avoid something in the road. The less you know them, the greater the distance you need to allow. As a guide, half a wheel to a wheel's length is ideal on flat or climbing terrain. As your speed increases, perhaps because of a descent, you will need to allow more room. On a fast descent, you will need to allow several bike lengths to maintain a safe distance.

Calls and Pointing

Most people within the group are unable to see the road surface and any obstacles ahead, such as parked cars or bollards within the road. This is why road cyclists have developed a set of calls and actions to instruct and inform following riders. These calls and actions are generally universal but may vary slightly from club to club or country to country (obviously language too!). The main calls and signals are:

"Car Up" – There's a car approaching the rear of the group. Be prepared to act and don't swing out to the side of the main group.

"Car Down" – There's a car approaching the front of the group. Be prepared to act and don't swing out to the side of the main group.

"Out!" – Often accompanied by a hand behind the back pointing to the direction of safety. This normally signifies a parked car or some other object you don't want to come into contact with.

"Line Out" – Riders to break formation and move into a single line. Typically used on climbs, high traffic areas or narrow carriageways where riding two abreast could be dangerous. Experienced riders will move from two abreast to single file in a smooth motion with riders on the outer edge of the road making room for the riders towards the centre of the road to slot into place.

"Middle" – there's a danger, such as a pothole, in the middle of the carriageway. Prepare to move out to the left or right.

"To your left/right" – said by a rider as they approach from behind to your left/right. This is to avoid surprising the rider in front and to ensure they don't make a sudden move.

"Standing" – said by a rider when climbing as they are about to stand. This is because as the rider stands, they momentarily loose pace and a rider close to their rear wheel may hit them.

"On your wheel" – said by a rider to let a rider upfront know that they now have someone riding close to their rear wheel. This is generally used when the rider up front may be unaware that a rider is about to take their wheel.

Although these are the most common calls, there are many variations such as "Lorry" or "Dog". However, once you know the basics, further variants are all pretty self-explanatory. You should also note that when the call is to signal a danger to the entire group, it is common practice for each rider to shout it so that it ripples back down through the group and everyone is aware of the issue.

Etiquette

Not only is there a specific lexicon for road cyclists, there is also an unwritten code of conduct. Knowing this code will enhance your riding experience and ensure that you don't inadvertently annoy other members of the group. The following, although not exhaustive, will help you avoid unintentional faux pas.

Hill bagging – a rider who does not share the workload at the front of the group and saves their energy to sprint to the top of climbs before other riders is known as a "hill bagger" – often known by far less savoury terms. Hill bagging is a guaranteed way to lose friends and become the least popular member of the group.

Take your turn – as mentioned earlier, it is harder work to ride at the front of a group than to ride within it. Take your turn and share the workload. If you genuinely don't have the strength, say and try again later during the ride.

Don't be a wheel hugger – similar to take your turn, but generally within a small group. No one appreciates someone sitting on their wheel watching them do all the work, especially on climbs.

Half wheeling – is when a rider sits behind another rider but allows their front wheel to overlap the front rider's rear wheel. It's dangerous and annoying for the rider up front.

Nose clearing – a lot of people can suffer from a build-up of mucus as they exercise. If you choose to clear this whilst riding, move to the side or preferably the rear of the group before doing so – no one appreciates being covered in snot!

Undertaking – professional riders pass each other on the left and the right, but they're massively experienced and not riding on open roads. Always pass people on the outside – undertaking is unexpected and can be dangerous.

Eating/drinking/changing clothing – from time to time you'll need to drink, eat or modify your clothing – for example, removing arm warmers or donning a race cape. When you perform these actions, you'll be sitting up and taking one or both hands off the handlebar. This compromises your ability to react to movements or changes of pace within the group. It follows that it's good form to move to the back of the group so that your actions don't endanger your fellow riders.

Loose cannons – you hope that everyone knows how to ride fluidly as a group, but from time to time you'll encounter riders whose actions are hard to predict and who make sudden and unexpected moves. These loose cannons can be dangerous or, at best, make you warier thus diminishing the enjoyment of your ride. Learn to spot loose cannons and avoid riding near them.

Punctures and mechanicals – from time to time people puncture or experience a problem with their bike. The correct procedure is to call out that you have a problem and carefully pull over to the side of the road. During social rides, all or some of the group will pull over and help the rider. On the other hand, in some instances such as fast rides, the group may continue and it's up to the affected rider to catch up with the group or make their way home solo.

Regrouping – as you've already discovered, the group breaks apart when riders tackle a climb. The following descent is normally a place for riders to regroup. Common etiquette is that faster riders freewheel or soft pedal to allow trailing riders to regroup, and that slower riders make a concerted effort to catch the leading riders.

Being dropped – when a slower rider loses contact with the main group, they have been dropped. All riders have been dropped at some point whether it's because they are not strong enough to stick with the group or they're just having a bad day. Most social rides aim to keep everyone together for the duration of the ride, but many other rides will see riders dropped. If you are dropped, don't worry - it happens. Enjoy the ride home and hope that you're in better shape for the next ride. If you constantly get dropped, you should consider moving to a slower group or finding different rides within which to participate.

Acknowledgements – normally when a rider passes another coming from the opposite direction, the riders acknowledge each other with a simple signal such as a hand raised from the handlebar or a nod of the head. You will, however, find that in areas where there are lots of cyclists, people simply don't bother acknowledging each other. There are no hard and fast rules of when and when not to acknowledge people – you just have to go based on feel.

Pacelines and Riding in Formation

During social rides, you'll find that the group of riders is quiet fluid with riders moving backwards or forwards within the group in an informal, unstructured way. When the tempo of a ride increases, or traffic conditions dictate a more structured approach, riders will form pacelines where they ride in a defined formation. Some pacelines are suited only to racing situations because the width of the group can become too great for legal and safe road riding. This chapter deals with the main types of paceline you are likely to encounter during club or group riding.

Single Paceline

The single pace line is the simplest of formations. As Figure 73 shows the riders ride in series with only a small gap between each rider. The rider at the front of the line takes the brunt of air resistance and does the most work. After doing their turn, the rider pulls off toward the centre of the road and slows their pace so that they slowly return to the rear of the group and that the second rider now takes the lead. If the group is travelling at speed or is fighting a strong headwind, the front rider may take a turn of as little as ten or fifteen seconds, whereas if the conditions are favourable and the pace moderate, the lead rider may take a turn of five or ten minutes.

Double Paceline

The double paceline is similar to the single paceline, but riders travel two abreast and, as Figure 74 illustrates, the front riders peel off one to each side of the line. This style of paceline provides a very social setup and makes a good formation for social rides. Before adopting the double paceline, it is important that the group assesses road and traffic conditions to ensure that it is safe and considerate to occupy an entire side of the carriageway.

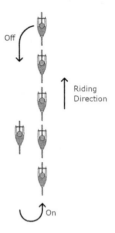

Figure 73 Single paceline

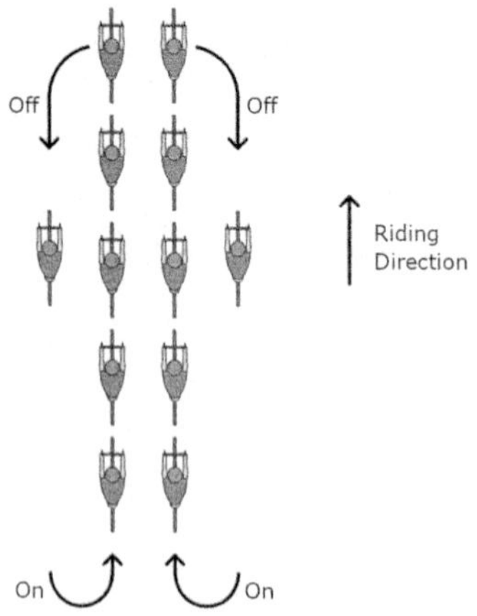

Figure 74 Double paceline

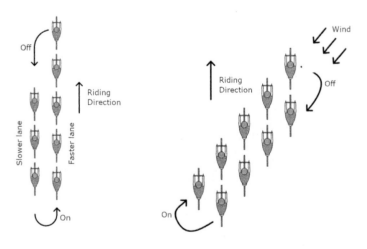

Figure 75 Through and off

Figure 76 Echelon

Through and Off

Many cycling clubs hold a weekly chain-gang which allows riders the opportunity to ride at pace in a structured manner. When riding within a chain-gang, each rider's turn on the front is just a few seconds until the next rider takes their turn. As Figure 75 illustrates, because each rider's turn is so short, the paceline actually consists of two lines where one is moving faster than the other. As the front rider of the faster line reaches the front of the formation, they move across to the slower line where they take a brief turn at the front until the next rider takes their place. Performed correctly, through and off becomes a fluid circular rotation of riders who are capable at moving at a high pace.

When riding in a through and off formation, it is particularly important to ride smoothly and avoid sudden accelerations and decelerations. Sudden changes in speed can either break the formation or cause an accident. If you are at the back of the line and can't take your turn, notify the rider in front with a call of "wheel" thus ensuring the smooth continuation of the paceline. Conversely, if you've moved off the slower line and moved to the rear of the faster line, call "last" as you start to pass the final rider in the slower ride, so that they can prepare to move out on to your wheel.

Echelon

The echelon is a formation that you should not use during normal group riding because it necessitates riders using a large amount of the carriageway. However, it is a particularly useful formation when riding with crosswinds during closed road events such as sportives. As Figure 76 illustrates, the riders form a staggered line where each rider helps protect the following rider from strong crosswinds whilst at the same time providing protection from frontal air resistance. When riding in a larger group, it is common for the group to split into multiple echelons because the width of the carriageway restricts the number of riders that can stay in formation. Notice how the front rider, in common with the single paceline, peels off to the side when they have completed their turn at the front of the group.

Rounding Up

In this chapter, you've discovered the many benefits of riding in a group. You then learnt the calls, signals and etiquette of group riding. Finally, you explored the formations and techniques for riding in pacelines and echelons.

Moving Forward: Your Next Steps

Now that you're becoming an experienced road cyclist, you might want to expand your riding repertoire from weekend rides with friends and the occasional commute to something more interesting or challenging. In this chapter, you'll discover a selection of activities that will add a new dimension and purpose to your riding. Try them out and discover what works for you, you never know until you try.

> "Just do what you love doing.
> That's my only advice."
>
> Peter Sagan

Cycling Clubs

Almost since the invention of the bike, people have come together and formed cycling clubs. They're a place where like-minded people can pursue a shared passion. Clubs focus on different aspects of cycling. Some are touring clubs, some invitation only elite racing clubs and others are general clubs focusing on a weekly ride and a collection of events throughout the year. Wherever you live, you'll find a general road cycling club nearby. To find a suitable club, either search the web or pop down to your local bike shop for a chat.

Most clubs have a weekend ride where members come together to ride. In many clubs these rides will be split into two or more levels depending on distance and pace, so you'll be certain there'll be a ride suitable for your level. Don't be shy. Contact the local club and ask where and when the meet-up is and check that there's a suitable level for your ability. Generally, clubs will allow you to ride as a guest, but they will expect you to become a member once you've gone on a few rides.

Once you've got into the swing of weekly group rides, you'll discover what else the club has to offer. This varies from club to club, but typical offerings (you'll discover more about these in this chapter) include:

- A time trial series.
- A racing scene or calendar.
- Spring training camps.
- A social calendar.
- Club appearances and participation in sportives and charity rides.
- Chain gang sessions.
- Hill climbs.

Joining a cycling club is one of the best things that you'll ever do in your new road cycling career. You'll enjoy the social element, you'll learn from old hands and you'll gain an invaluable source of inspiration to keep pedalling during cold dark winter days. Go on, get out there this weekend – you're more ready than you think!

Figure 77 A club outing

Time Trialling

People take part in cycle time trials all over the world, but their origins lie in Victorian England. In 1890 as the road racing scene started to build steam and develop across Europe, the National Cyclists' Union banned racing on public roads in Britain. In response, would-be-racers would hold secret meetings at night without lights and all dressed in black (that's why UK cyclists are so fond of black clothing) to avoid detection by the authorities. They would then hold 'races' where each rider would set off in turn with a small time gap separating each rider. The rider who recorded the fastest time won the event. The general principal hasn't changed to this day, but riders now meet in daylight and events are compliant with the law.

> **Good to Know:** In the UK you don't need to hold a race licence or take a medical to take part in time trials. It is, however, wise to ensure that the event provides appropriate insurance.

Time trialling is one of most inclusive forms of cycle racing that exists. It doesn't matter if you're young or old, fit or unfit, slim or carrying a few additional pounds, you can still compete. You are racing against the clock and, ultimately, against yourself. After your first event you might clock 30 minutes for ten miles (btw, the current record is 16 mins 35 secs), so the next time you'll aim to better this and maybe you'll make 29 minutes. When you first start time trialling, your gains are huge - you'll knock minutes off your times within weeks. Of course, there's still a sense of competition and rivalry at events. You'll soon see that there are other riders with similar times to yours. It's only natural to push that little bit harder to try and better their time – you can be sure that they'll do the same.

Time trials take place over many distances, but the most popular are ten and twenty-five miles at a club level. Larger events known as 'opens' are often held at 10, 25, 50 and 100 miles, although other distances do exist. For those that really like to suffer, there are 12 and 24-hour events where the winner is the person that accumulates the greatest distance in the given time. As a matter of interest, the current records are:

> *12 Hour: A. Wilkinson 317.87 miles*
>
> *24 Hour: A. Wilkinson 541.17 miles*

Needless to say, Andy Wilkinson is a legendary figure in the world of time trialling and has set many records over his career.

Once you've competed in a few time trials, you're likely to get the bug for it and want to improve your times. Training and taking part in events will form the foundation of your gains but you will also notice that there's a lot of specialised equipment available for both rider and bike. All of this equipment is designed to make the rider and bike more aerodynamic and therefore, faster. For now, ride on the drops (see Rolling: First Pedal Strokes chapter) and ride harder than you can believe, suffer much and remember the adage:

"Pain is only weakness leaving the body!"

Anon

Road Racing

The first recorded cycling race was in 1868 and it took place in Paris, France. Unfortunately for the French, it was won by an Englishman James Moore. Almost immediately after this first race, cycle road racing became a popular activity throughout Europe and shortly after in the USA, with its first race being held in 1878 in Boston. The most famous of all road races, the

Figure 78 Time trialling - the ultimate test

Tour de France, was first held in 1903 when the L'Auto (now L'Equipe) newspaper devised the idea of creating and staging a brutal cycle race in an attempt to sell more newspapers. Since these early races, road racing has grown from strength to strength and it is now practiced at all levels in numerous countries.

Today, in the US and UK (and other countries, naturally) there is a strong amateur racing scene. Local events are held up and down the countries on a regular basis and many of these are open to any licenced riders. In the UK, British Cycling issues licences and there's another organisation, TLI Cycling, but this restricts riders to TLI Cycling domestic events. In the US, USA Cycling issues licences. A new rider starts as a Cat 4 and accumulates points as they achieve results. To attain the next category, a rider must accumulate a certain number of points. Amateur racers hope to move from Cat 4 up to Cat 1, although few achieve this level. Different races are open to different categories of riders so as to allow riders to compete with those of a similar ability. So, when you start off, you'll race mostly in Cat 4 races or Cat 3/4 (two categories combined) events. Races, especially in the lower categories, are often held on circuits closed to the public. You'll learn more about this in the next section of this chapter.

"The race is won by the rider who can suffer the most."

Eddy Merckx

Racing is hard at any level, but it is also a great way to give your riding a purpose. You'll soon find that you start to train more specifically as you are driven to gain better results, or to beat someone that always just seems to have the edge on you. When you first start, don't be discouraged if shortly after the race starts, you are dropped from the peloton – it's part of the learning process. You will improve!

Criterium Racing

Technically, road racing takes place on open roads with a road closure, or rolling road closure, over a given distance whereas criterium racing takes places on a closed circuit that is often in the region of a mile in length and where riders race for multiple laps of the circuit. Nowadays, because of the cost and safety considerations of racing on the open road, many 'road races' are in effect held as criteriums.

Figure 79 Preparing for the race

The normal format for a criterium is for riders to race around a circuit for a given amount of time plus 'x' laps. For example, one hour plus three laps is a commonly adopted format. The circuits may be situated on an industrial estate, a motor racing circuit or, at a high-level, within a closed city centre. Wherever the race is held, they are characterised by rapid accelerations and heavy braking as riders enter and exit each corner on the circuit. Once you try this style of racing you'll discover a new world of pain and exhilaration that you never knew existed: your legs scream, your heart beats at an almost inconceivable rate, your lungs gasp and pulse in your chest and at the end of it all, you'll walk away with a smile and not be able to stop talking about the race until the next one.

Sportives

If you love the idea of road racing but hate the idea of all the pain and training, sportives could be for you. Sportives are mass participation cycling events held over a variety of distances ranging from a leisurely twenty miles to more than one hundred miles in mountainous territory. Smaller events have mass starts, whereas larger events that may have thousands of riders, see riders leave in waves. The great thing about a sportive is you can make it personal. Some riders are happy to have a leisurely day out with company, others view an event as a personal challenge (perhaps their first century) and others will want to achieve the fastest time possible and treat it like a road race. Whatever your intentions, you'll end up riding with a group of people of a similar ability so there's plenty of fun to be had.

> **Good to Know:** Cyclists refer to 100 miles as a century. Completing your first century is a major milestone as you develop as a cyclist.

There are many differing organisers and styles of event. Many cycling clubs will host an annual sportive that showcases their local riding and climbs. These tend to be good value for money and have an informal vibe. Then there are commercial events, where riders receive goody bags, official times, souvenirs such as t-shirts and a lot of support in terms of food, drink and mechanical assistance. Commercial events are far more expensive than locally organized events. Finally, there are classic events where entry can be hard to attain and many of which appear on riders' bucket lists. For example, the following events are all hugely popular and oversubscribed each year:

- Fred Whitton Challenge (England) notorious 180 km ride with horrendous climbs.
- Etape Caledonia (Scotland) 130 km of closed roads, infamous for course sabotage in 2009.
- Tour of Wessex (England) a three-day event covering 512 km.
- Ride London (England).
- Paris Roubaix (Belgium & France) up to 172 km where you can experience the wheel crunching pavé that the pro's ride.
- Mallorca 312 (Spain) up to 312 km in a single day with plenty of mountains thrown in to make things harder.
- Etape de Tour (France) an actual stage of the Tour de France, location and terrain varies each year.
- Tour of California Experience like the Etape de Tour but for the Tour of California.
- Cape Town Cycle Tour the world's biggest timed bike race.

Whatever your reason for riding, a sportive will give you an unforgettable experience. Find and enter some events and you'll add a new dimension to your riding as you train towards a specific goal.

Charity Rides

Charity rides are really a variant on sportives, but the focus is on raising money for charity whether that's through entrance fees or individual sponsorship. You will find that some, but certainly not all, charity rides cover shorter distances than other sportives and attract cyclists that are far more recreationally focused – they are one of the only events where you may see folding and shopping bikes alongside racing bikes! Some of the better-known events include:

- NSPCC London to Paris: a five-day ride from the centre of London to the Eiffel Tower, Paris.

- British Heart Foundation London to Brighton Night Ride: a 60-mile ride that adds an altruistic element to the long-established London to Brighton Bike Ride.

- UK End to End: a gruelling 1000-mile 10-day event covering the length of the UK.

Spring Training Camps

For many cyclists, the winter seems to last an eternity. Months of cold, damp weather leave you dreaming of the sun kissing your legs, spinning effortlessly with the sunshine on your back and relaxing in the warmth with the cool of a chilled beer. So it is then that every year, thousands of cyclists from amateurs to professionals take off on a spring training camp.

For some, the spring training camp marks the transition between winter miles and a new season's racing. These riders will search out serious mileage and aim to sharpen their legs to become race ready. For others, the spring training camp offers a more social event where they can spin their legs and enjoy local food and drink whilst escaping the misery of winter. Whatever your reason for going you'll find that spring training camps fall into two distinct categories:

1. Club or self-organised

2. Commercial training camps

Most cycling clubs will either formally, or informally, organize a spring getaway. Going with your club allows you to benefit from members' knowledge of places to stay, bike rental or shipping and routes in the local area. On the other hand, commercial training camps offer structured programmes based on ability with expert guides to show you routes away from the crowds of other cyclists. These camps will often organise and

197

manage things such as cycle hire or shipping, accommodation and repairs or mechanical assistance.

Figure 80 A well earned beer

One of the great things about spring training is that it often involves going to tourist resorts outside of the main season, so prices tend to be very reasonable. Some of the most popular locations include:

- Mallorca: With over a quarter of a million cyclists visiting this island each year, and its stunning terrain that allows coast to mountain riding every day, it's no wonder that it's the number one destination for spring riding.
- Costa Blanca: Between Alicante and Valencia, there's a mild dry climate in winter that attracts many pro teams and plenty of amateurs too. There's plenty of climbing to test your legs and it's cheap to stay.

- Canary Islands: Both Tenerife and Gran Canaria host pro teams each year and they offer consistently warm dry weather throughout the year.

- Tuscany: Spain is not the only location in Europe to attract the pro's. Tuscany offers beautiful countryside, an inviting climate and plenty of climbing.

Good to Know: In countries where people drive and ride on the left-hand side of the road, the right-hand brake lever controls the front brake. Conversely, in countries where you ride on the right-hand side of the road, the left-hand lever controls the front brake. If you are hiring a bike in a country where people cycle on the opposite side, request in advance that the shop switches the brakes around. Many shops will do this for no additional charge. Equally, in some areas catering for the UK market, shops supply bikes setup for UK riders as standard.

Mountain Jaunts

You've enjoyed a spring training camp, shown off your newly acquired leg tan and got back into the day-to-day of cycling on your local roads. After a few months, you'll start to yearn for something a little more exotic – a place to test your new-found fitness and strength. It has to be the mountains. As you discovered in the "Climbing" section, nothing tests a road rider more than a good mountain ascent. Each year, thousands of cyclists leave home and head to Europe's mountains to test themselves on the climbs that the professionals make light work of during the grand tours of France, Spain and Italy.

Summer in the mountains is magical. It's so beautiful, often peaceful, and the only places where you'll find the most testing and enduring of climbs. Many of winter's ski resorts re-open their doors to greet cyclists (road and mountain) each summer season. You'll find that prices in these resorts tend to be lower than in the winter season, so a mountain holiday need not be an expensive affair. You can ride in all the big mountain chains such as the Alps, the Pyrenees and the Dolomites though you will find that road cycling activity concentrates on the areas most synonymous with the grand tours, notably:

- Bourg-d'Oisans: A pretty town that provides access to mythical climbs such as L'Alpe d'Huez, Col du Galibier, Col de la Croix de Fer and Col de la Madeleine.
- Mont Ventoux: The Giant of Provence is isolated from the other notable climbs but is so iconic that every road cyclist needs to climb it at least once (btw there are three routes to the summit so perhaps you need to climb it three times!). Three main towns serve cyclists wanting to tackle the Giant: Bedoin (start point for most famous ascent), Malaucène and Sault.
- Morzine: A base that provides access to several well-known Tour de France climbs such as Col de Joux Plane, Col de la Joux Verte, Col de la Ramaz and Morzine-Avoriaz. Morzine also offers an excellent location for trying your hand at downhill mountain biking with an impressive selection of lift networks, runs for all abilities and bike and equipment hire.
- Briançon: A base for taking on Col d'Izoard and many other climbs such as Col du Granon, Col du Galibier and Sestriere.

Triathlon & Duathlon

For some people, riding a bike is simply not enough – they need to suffer more. If you enjoy running or swimming, perhaps triathlon or duathlon might be your thing. Triathlons take the format of swim-bike-run and duathlons run-bike-run. Both disciplines adopt a variety of lengths and all are incredibly popular. Table 5 shows the standard lengths of triathlon events:

Event	Swim (Miles)	Cycle (Miles)	Run (Miles)
Sprint	0.5	15	3
Olympic	0.93	24.8	6.2
Half Ironman	1.2	56	13
Ironman	2.4	112	26.2 (Marathon)

Table 5 Common triathlon distances

Combining events pushes greater stresses on your body. You may think that a 25-mile cycle is nothing, but after a mile swim, with your heart in your mouth, you'll find it a very different experience. Getting started in triathlon is simple – practice riding, swimming and running then enter an event. Becoming good requires focused training in all three disciplines and the fourth discipline – transition, the period when you switch from one discipline to another.

If you find triathlon is for you, you'll be pleased to know that there are numerous local clubs where you'll be able to train and socialise with like-minded individuals. As a bonus, you'll still be welcome at your local cycling club but, be warned, don't start riding with triathlon clothing (see the "What not to Wear" section of the "Selecting the Right Gear: What to Wear" chapter).

Hill Climbs

Hill climbs are a specialist type of time trial where you race up a hill as fast as possible. Many cycling clubs organise their own annual hill climb events often at the end of the summer season before winter arrives. There are several high-profile events for those that are really serious and talented. If you're a mountain goat, this could be your ideal event. Start with local club events and then search online for bigger events.

Holidays

There's a growing trend that builds on spring training camps and mountain jaunts - the organised cycling holiday. There are numerous companies that specialise in providing cycling holidays. These holidays cater for cyclists of all abilities from those that take an occasional recreational ride to those that are serious racing cyclists. Many companies specialise in long-haul breaks where route options, accommodation, rider support and meals are all organized on your behalf. Expert local knowledge can help ensure that you explore the best an area has to offer without adopting a trial and error approach where you plan everything yourself. Not only does this make rides potentially more satisfying, it can also make them safer if you choose to ride in less familiar areas such as South America or the Far East. Before you book a holiday, ensure that you are realistic about your own abilities. If you choose a break that has too slow a pace, you'll soon become frustrated whereas if you choose too great a pace or duration, you'll exhaust yourself and the enjoyment of the experience will soon pass.

Rounding Up

In this chapter, you've explored several activities that can add depth and further meaning to your road riding. You also learnt how cycling clubs can enrich your riding experience and allow you to learn from more experienced riders.

Final Thoughts

This book has guided you from being a non-cyclist through to one who is knowledgeable and able to ride confidently on any terrain whether solo or as part of a group. In the future as you progress, you'll find that certain aspects of road cycling will fire your imagination and enthusiasm. Whatever your next steps, you'll find that there's a whole treasure trove of materials (video, literature and courses) to help you on your journey. I truly hope that your journey brings you joy, excitement and many new friends and that one day, I'll see you out on some continental road. Until then, as a parting gift, I offer the words of Greg LeMond, three times winner of the Tour de France:

"It never gets easier; you just go faster."

Greg LeMond

Acknowledgements

The original intention behind this book was to share knowledge and help people new to the sport that I love so much. As I progressed through the writing phase, I met more and more people who were enthused by the idea and many of whom subsequently offered their help and assistance. I'd particularly like to thank the people without whose help this book would not have been possible. So, in no particular order:

Mike Astle – An avid cyclist, Ironman and photographer. Little did you know that living the dream in Mallorca would see you hanging and diving out of cars in the pursuit of the perfect shot. Thanks so much for your photography, which has brought this book to life.

https://www.instagram.com/asty121/

Simon Roxburgh – a fanatic cyclist, triathlete, former Welsh Standard Distance Age Group Champion and my little brother. Thank you for modelling in the photo shoots, for casting a critical eye over this book's content and for introducing me to the cycling delights of Mallorca.

Rhian Roxburgh – an exceptional triathlete and an inspiration on the bike. Two times ETU Triathlon European Champion and bronze medallist in the World Age Group Championships. Rhian is the founder of TriRox Training. Thank you for the photo opportunities and getting me back on the bike all those years ago.

http://www.triroxtraining.co.uk

Ryan Mullen – Ryan rides for Trek-Segafredo and is two times Irish National Road Champion and three times Irish National Time Trial Champion. Thank you for giving your time during the run up to the Giro and for showing us how to look good on a bike.

Dan Evans – Dan (Assos-Equipe UK) is twice RTTC Hill Climb Champion. Thank you for letting us chase you around Mallorca capturing some quality photographic moments.

https://www.instagram.com/danevanscycling/

Jane Astle – A busy communications executive who when not working, loves to get out on the bike and enjoy all that Mallorca has to offer. It was so generous of you to give up your time to proof-read and work your magic on this book.

Rachel James-Owens – My co-pilot, triathlete and mountain biker. Thank you for being a reviewer and being my sounding board. If you had not cracked the whip, I might have never finished this book.

George Wainwright and the team at Pope & Wainwright - your strategic design consultancy delivered the icing on the cake - a cover that perfectly encapsulates the essence of road cycling. Thank you so much.

http://www.popewainwright.com

I'd also like to thank the reviewers of this book, whose comments and thoughts have created a more rounded and inclusive offering. So, thank you: Graham Burns, Malcolm Coles, Andrew Grundy, Andy Little and Esther Purdy.

Finally, I'd like to thank all the cyclists young and old, fast and slow, amateur or professional whose riding during the Mallorcan winter days provided me with the inspiration to keep on writing.

Further Reading

Associations

There are numerous associations and organisations dedicated to specific elements of cycling. The following are those that are mentioned within this book.

- British Cycling
  www.britishcycling.org.uk
- British Triathlon Federation
  www.britishtriathlon.org
- Cycling Time Trials
  www.cyclingtimetrials.org.uk
- Sustrans
  www.sustrans.org.uk
- TLI Cycling
  www.tlicycling.org.uk

Events

The following events are mentioned earlier in this book and are certainly worth checking out. For many of the point to point rides, namely London-Brighton, London-Paris, UK end to end, you will find that there are several organisers promoting a number of events. The inclusion of an event here is not a specific recommendation, simply a link to a popular event.

- Amgen Tour of California Experience
  www.trainright.com/bucket-list/events/
- Cape Town Cycle Tour
  www.capetowncycletour.com
- Deloitte Ride Across Britain
  www.rideacrossbritain.com
- Etape Caledonia
  www.etapecaledonia.co.uk
- L'Etape du Tour
  www.letapedutour.com
- London to Brighton Bike Ride
  www.bhf.org.uk/L2B
- London to Paris
  www.londonparisbikeride.co.uk
- Mallorca 312
  www.mallorca312.com
- Paris Roubaix Challenge
  www.parisroubaixchallenge.com
- Prudential Ride London
  www.prudentialridelondon.co.uk
- The Saddleback Fred Whitton Challenge
  www.fredwhittonchallenge.co.uk
- Tour of Wessex
  www.pendragonsports.com/Tour_of_Wessex
- World Naked Bike Ride
  www.worldnakedbikeride.org

Holidays and Travel

The following websites are the official websites for the cycling locations mentioned earlier in this book.

- Bourg d'Oisans
  bourgdoisans.com/en/leisures/road-cycling

- Briançon
  www.serre-chevalier.com/en/summer/activities/cycling/
- Costa Blanca
  www.costablanca.org/esp/cyclingcb
- Grand Canaria
  www.grancanaria.com/turismo/en/nature/mountain-sports/cycling/
- Info Mallorca
  www.infomallorca.net/?te=sec&e=17064
- Morzine
  www.morzinemountaincycling.com/en/index.html
- Mount Ventoux (Bedoin)
  gb.bedoin.org/
- Tenerife
  www.webtenerife.co.uk/what-to-do/sports/land/cycling
- Tuscany
  www.visittuscany.com/en/theme/cycling/

Table of Figures

All photography except Figure 20 copyright Mike Astle. Figure 20 and illustrations copyright Peter Roxburgh.

About the Author

Peter learned to ride horses and bikes when he was two. Horses were great for attracting girls but bikes meant freedom. As he got older, he found that there were other ways to get a girl so he stopped riding horses. The more time he spent with girls, the more he realised he needed to keep a bike. Nowadays, he has three girls in his life: his partner, his daughter and his granddaughter. Naturally with all those girls, he has several bikes which he rides wherever there's great cycling, food, and weather.

  @roxramblings